CRIEFF HYDRO

CRIEFF HYDRO

GUY CHRISTIE

Published by Crieff Hydro Limited

First Published 1967
Revised 1986

ISBN 0 95118620 5

© STRATHEARN HYDROPATHIC ESTABLISHMENT CO. LTD.

Printed in Great Britain by
MᶜCorquodale (Scotland) Ltd.

ACKNOWLEDGEMENTS

Crieff Hydropathic is like a magnet. Visitors who come to know it return time and again to enjoy a "refresher course". To many of those *habitués* I am indebted for facts *and* fiction regarding the regime and the House—Strathearn House, the Establishment, or, more affectionately and simply, The Hydro. My sincere thanks are due, also, to a number of others who have assisted in no small degree in what has turned out to be a work of some complexity.

Mr John Leckie, the Manager, has been a source of much information and help, always willing to listen to my difficulties and queries; and to his fellow-director, Sir Malcolm Knox, I am equally grateful for valuable suggestions.

Older members of the staff, I hope, will find some reflections of their talks with me, and I have had constant co-operation from Mr David Philips, Editor of the *Strathearn Herald*.

To all these and to Mr J. M. King, Edinburgh, for useful and kindly criticism; Mr G. Campbell H. Paton, Edinburgh, and Mr James Paton, Carnoustie, for factual help; the Rev. Dr D. P. Thomson, Crieff, for helpful interest; Mr J. H. Stewart and Miss Catherine L. Dickson, of the Central Reference Library, Edinburgh; and Mr A. D. MacLeod and staff of the Registrar General's Office, Edinburgh, I am most grateful for guidance so willingly given.

I have to acknowledge, further, kind permission given by the following to use extracts from the books named:

Mr A. R. B. Haldane, author of *The Drove Roads of Scotland*, published by Thos. Nelson and Sons Ltd.

The Porpoise Press (Faber and Faber Ltd.)—*I Remember* by J. J. Bell.

George Allen and Unwin Ltd.—*Constance Louisa Maynard* by C. B. Firth.

Wyman Marshall Ltd.—*The Rise and Progress of Hydropathy in England and Scotland* by Richard Metcalfe.

Oliphants Ltd.—*History of Crieff* by Alexander Porteous.

The Hydro, October, 1985

FOREWORD

The history of Crieff Hydro was written in 1968 by Guy Christie, and published as part of the celebrations to commemorate the centenary of the business, when my uncle, the late J. R. Donaldson, was Chairman of the Company.

Much has happened since then. For many of to-day's guests the events recorded in that first edition are indeed history, and depict a world that has greatly changed, for then the Hydro was without chalets, the Sports Hall, or purpose built conference facilities.

The book too, has been out of print for some years—but is still regularly asked for—and so we have resolved to publish a second edition, adding a chapter describing the developments of the last twenty years.

Though much has changed we believe that the tradition and atmosphere of the Hydro continue to reflect the aims so firmly established by Dr Meikle, and we hope that the story will be read with pleasure by a new generation of Hydro guests and friends.

G. N. DONALDSON
Chairman

Crieff
July 1986

CONTENTS

VIGNETTE

The scene is a sunlit one, for the place is Northern Italy in May. Sitting out on the balcony of a holiday-de-luxe hotel that overlooks the Lake of Como, blue and shimmering in the heat, though the hour is only breakfast-time, are a couple, the man putting as cheerful a face on his continental breakfast as possible; his lady enraptured by the unaccustomed heat as well as by the view. She sighs with contentment and looks at her husband. He swallows the last of his "croissant", wipes the crumbs off his fingers, and leans back in his chair.

"Do you realise," he says with great relish and solemnity, "that in thirteen weeks we will be at Crieff Hydro?"

"HOME FROM HOME"

Blest be that spot, where cheerful guests retire
To pause from toil, and trim their evening fire;
Blest that abode, where want and pain repair,
And every stranger find a ready chair.

Crieff Hydro—or just "Crieff" to the great majority of its guests—is in many ways without an equal. The sentence "I am made all things to all men" seems particularly appropriate to this establishment on the completion of its hundredth year in 1968. It has been a place of comfort, of good service and of happiness to the thousands of visitors who have come year after year, in summer and in winter, from its inception. It is not easy to decide whether the friendly atmosphere which pervades the Hydro emanates from the walls, the staff or the guests, but it certainly is felt by the individuals and the families who like to return to it generation after generation, and who have so many mutual interests that friendship, fun and happiness come easily. Few days can pass when there is not present among the guests someone who has as a child spent part of his holidays at the Hydro. Who knows how many met their wives or husbands here or enjoyed their honeymoon at Crieff?

One of Scotland's largest hotels, the Hydro has never had a bar, never tried to attract tourists, scarcely ever advertised itself and yet has gone from strength to strength. Although Dr Thomas Henry Meikle, the founder, set a standard of modernity, so that the establishment has been in many respects ahead of its time, the management has always been composed of amateurs in hotel-keeping. They have been doctors of medicine, civil servants, graduates in agriculture and despite the diversity of their backgrounds, a feature of the Hydro's history has been that its outlook and image have remained strikingly constant. Two features these men have shared have been a family tie with old Dr Meikle in every case and a strong but practical

Presbyterianism. The unique position which the Hydro holds in the hotel world to-day is linked with these facts.

To set the back cloth to the "Hydro atmosphere", let us stroll out to the forecourt and watch some of the arrivals. A car comes round the corner of the building, laden to the roofrack. It rolls up with assurance for it had been here before and comes to a halt inside the "No Parking" area. A porter appears with a large trolley, he greets the family by name and without further ado off-loads mountains of luggage, golf clubs, tennis and badminton rackets, riding hats and crops and even skis. While this is going on, the family is looking around.

"There are the Smiths", says Father.

One of the children yells at a boy standing near the tennis courts, while his embarrassed sister tells him not to make so much noise and her eyes cast round to see if Peter (or Tom or George) is in the vicinity. All but father who goes to park the car then disappear towards the reception.

The next family to arrive have not been before and they are more subdued. They enter the hall in a body, preceded by a porter. They pause with some wonderment as they see the spacious ballroom and the winter garden and are surprised by the length of the corridor. They wonder where their rooms are, when lunch is served and, in general—are they going to enjoy themselves? They need not fear, for the company in the Hydro seems to coalesce into a fellow-ship, and the atmosphere is that of a large family—with more tolerance and good humour than in many families. Of course there are likes and dislikes, harmony and disharmony. Remember that for at least six months out of twelve there are between 300 and 400 people living under one roof. Remember too, that the picture changes almost completely every fortnight or so as new arrivals flow in and their predecessors leave. But all the tributes, the innumerable expressions of delight and approval go to show how genuine and universal is this fellowship.

Look again at our arrivals on the Saturday of their departure and the mood is very different. Father is en-grossed in the serious problem of cramming an enlarged collection of luggage into a groaning car. Mother is fussing inside the Hydro, because her erring children are nowhere to be found. Sister is lost in the crowd of well-wishers snapping their last photo of the "Gang" and younger brother has escaped to the pool for his last dip. Finally, an hour later than a carefully planned schedule, the family, are buckled into the car, farewells are complete and the parting shout is "See you next year".

THE PLEASANT VOICES

"Still are thy pleasant voices, thy nightingales awake;
For Death, he taketh all away, but them he cannot take."
CORY

So strongly has the Hydropathic left its mark upon its inhabitants that we have evidence of thousands of words written in letters, books and newspapers about it.

In order that we may see what the establishment was like at the beginning of its life, we must delve into the pages of this literature.

Quite the earliest note on the Hydro from the pen of a visitor is to be found in a biography entitled *Constance Louisa Maynard*, by C. B. Firth. In July 1876, Constance Maynard, diarist and author, and later Principal of Westfield College in the University of London, accompanied her brother George, who, apparently, was often ailing, to Crieff Hydropathic, then in its eighth year. They had sailed from London to Leith, and spent a couple of days in St. Andrews where, the following year, Miss Maynard was to take up teaching when the new girls' school of St. Leonard's opened.

Brother and sister arrived at the Hydro, and she writes:

"The House itself immensely large, airy and comfortable—some 130 visitors of every shade but [what virtue in 'but'?] nearly all Scotch, and the 30 neat housemaids and bathmaids who come into prayers are a sight. Out in the grounds, then some music in the fine large drawing room, and a scientific man, Mr Barker, gave a little lecture on the discoveries of the spectroscope."

That extract is from her diary. Her biographer goes on:

"George settled in at once for his treatment. The surroundings were satisfactory. Meals were served with clockwork regularity, 'with a fine of 1d. if late for Grace'. Among the 130 visitors, congenial spirits were soon discovered. Even 18 to 20 'Glasgow men', who came for the week-end—not that the

Diary uses the term—and sat together at table, 'appeared to spend a very creditable Scotch Sabbath'. Constance felt after some days that she could leave George without misgiving, though he promised to be 'amusingly miserable'."

Some idea of the place and the people emerges from those few sentences, but the picture is filled out by the enthusiastic eulogium of an American woman who stayed in Strathearn House for quite a time during the summer of 1904. Her account of her experiences appeared first in an American newspaper and this was copied by the *Strathearn Herald*, Crieff's local paper, on 4th November of that year.

AN AMERICAN'S OPINION

of

Crieff's Great Health Resort

Beautiful Place Near the Foot of the Grampian Hills, where Cleanliness and Godliness are prescribed Together.

Chimes Ring during Meal-Time, and Long Prayers Succeed Dessert—Prominent New York State Club Woman Likes the Experience.

(By Mrs Frederick L. Charles)

The above headings are given to the following article taken from a recent number of an American newspaper with reference to the Strathearn Hydropathic Establishment, Crieff:

We, Mrs Rose and I, are in Crieff, near the foot of the Grampian Hills, on the southern face of a wooded hill called The Knock. John Brown says "there is not in all Scotland, or, as far as I have seen in all else, a more exquisite twelve miles of scenery than that between Crieff and the foot of Loch Earn"; and Charles Reade has said—"The habitable globe possesses no more delightful spot than Crieff". I cannot say more than Mr Reade has said about Crieff, but I must write you some few things about this Strathearn Hydropathic Establishment, known as Strathearn House, where we are now living.

It is built high on a hill on a commanding plateau, in a sheltered site, and has all the signs of a palace. As soon as one approaches the place she sees "Private Grounds" staring her in the face, but once on the inside of the grounds she feels the estate is hers. The road from the Caledonian Station to the house is a winding one all the way up the hill, and a good steep climb it is, too. As one enters the grounds at Strathearn she is driven around and around alluring paths, before a view of the house can be seen. Strathearn is a tremendous establishment, equal to 500 guests. In order to become a guest of the house, one must come armed with a recommend from some friend of Dr Meikle, the owner, else she would stand small chance of getting accommodation, as the house is filled to the echo all the year round, on account of the climate and varied attractiveness of Crieff's scenery. There are sixty acres of cultivated gardens and forests for the use of guests. The house is actually sheltered by the "Knock of Crieff", a wooded hill of old red sandstone, which is about one thousand feet high. The view is unequalled, including all kinds of shifting scenes about the valley of the Earn and the mountain ranges beyond. There are enough walks about the place to satisfy pedestrians, also well defined trails leading to all the surrounding hills.

Now to the inside life of Strathearn, which I feel sure will interest Americans. We cannot decide whether we are in a boarding-school or theological training-house. We must do everything at a stated hour, and exactly as we are told. For instance, at seven o'clock in the morning the great bell in the tower rings. At fifteen minutes after seven all the chimes in all of the corridors are set playing; then at eight o'clock another set of well-tuned bells actually toll. The first bell is a signal to wake up; the second one announces hot water in little tin jugs at your door; the third says get dressed for breakfast. Then at 8.30 a solemn kind of gong is sounded, which for all the world sounds like the Angelus, and one feels infinitely more like bowing her head in prayer than like rushing pell-mell to the dining-room, where there are three rather long tables with 120 guests at each table. All are seated by the tap of a bell, and everyone must think "Amen" to a grace said by the house minister, or by some honoured guest who wears the cloth of the favourite Scotch profession. Men are ones to ask the blessing. I think we shall not be called upon, as women over here are listeners for the most part. Once up to breakfast, we are served to oatmeal porridge, well cooked, and milk—no cream, except on Wednesdays and Sundays; molasses and all kinds of breads, marmalade, bacon, eggs, coffee (very bad), and excellent tea.

At nine o'clock every guest is expected to go to the drawing-room for prayers. All the servants go, and if any guests come into breakfast late, and are not finished eating by nine o'clock, they are left to wait upon themselves, while the servants pray for the guests' late habits. The house organist plays a hymn on the big organ, the guests are on one side of the room, the servants the other, and all sing the hymn with great zeal. The chosen minister steps into the pulpit, after which everybody falls to his or her knees and listens to a long-drawn-out and fervent prayer for everything under the heavens in general, and for King Edward in particular. The ruler of these islands seems to need much praying for. Prayer over with, each goes her own way till time for luncheon, when the music of the various and beautiful bells begins to instruct the guests what to do at luncheon time. At four in the afternoon tea is served in the winter garden room, which is immense, and is all enclosed in glass, and furnished throughout in green and red wicker furniture. It is the most beautiful winter garden I have seen anywhere. Dinner is on at eight o'clock, and then a longer session of prayer follows the heavy meal. Immediately after prayers the young people retire to the dancing-room and whirl about till 10.30, when all the lights are turned off and sleep is in order.

Strathearn House is North Britain's most favourite resort. We two are the only American guests, and we secured rooms through the kindness of our friend, Miss Adam, of Bowden House. The Londoners, Edinburgh and Glasgow citizens make up the congregation. We enjoy it all so keenly that we are going to stay on so long as we can keep our rooms. Meantime we shall make up the excursions by carriage to Drummond Castle, Sma' Glen, Monzie Castle, Abercairny and other places. It is a great privilege to be here. You will notice it is not a house conducted exactly as we Americans manage our own resorts. I suppose a hydropathic establishment is more like our sanitoriums, since it furnishes all the waters, baths, and essentials to health, free of charge to the fortunate guests. The noticeable difference is the atmosphere which permeates the "hydro". The Scotchman looks to the spiritual as well as the physical health.

This revelation of conditions and routine in the House is a most valuable, social document, and one of the most lucid and penetrating we have.

Mrs Charles exaggerates somewhat at various points.

The Hydro has never accommodated 500 guests, the present figure being around 370. Once, at New Year, a long time ago, there were actually 399 guests and 70 servants in the House. She was most fortunate to enjoy the winter garden, for it had been completed only at Easter of that year, although it had been partially used during the New Year holidays. "Much appreciated and admired", states the Directors' minute of that spring. There are one or two discrepancies, but on the whole it is remarkably accurate, and the description of the ringing of the bells for meals, prayers, and in the mornings, is most vivid.

The penny fine, imposed for being late for meals, she does not mention. Constance Maynard and J. J. Bell speak of it, but perhaps by the time Mrs Charles stayed at the Hydro it had been done away with. The box in which the fines had to be placed is still in possession of the Manager, but it was not brought as a production in an astonishing case heard by the First Division of the Court of Session, Scotland's highest legal Court, with Lord President Inglis presiding. (John Inglis was the defending counsel in the famous trial of Madeleine Smith and succeeded, when she was charged with murder, in securing a verdict of "Not proven".)

This case was brought in 1881 under the Taxes Management Act of 1880, and involved a sum of £12 2s. 6d., the assessment which commissioners for Crieff district of Perthshire had decided to levy on the Hydro, being inhabited-house duty at the rate of 9d. in the £1, instead of 6d., the latter being the rate for hotels and inns. The commissioners were of opinion that the Company were not carrying on the business of hotelkeeper within the meaning of the Act, and one of their arguments was that no hotelkeeper could fine his guests 1d. in the way the appellants did. The rateable value of the Hydro at that time was £970.

The official Court of Session document summarising the case stated in one clause:

"The patients and visitors are subject to the strict rules of the establishment. They are rung up in the morning at a fixed hour. The meals are served only at certain fixed hours, and any inmate sitting down to table after grace is said, or making allusion to hydropathic treatment during meals, is fined. Family worship is held morning and evening. The front door is locked at 10.30 p.m., and the gas turned off at eleven p.m., when perfect quietness must be maintained by all.

"By the rules and regulations of the Company, which are hung up in the bedrooms of the establishment, for the information of the public, the officials of the Company are empowered to refuse admission and to send away such as they judge unsuitable. No children under six years of age are admitted, except under special arrangement."

I may say that the fine for alluding to hydropathic treatment during meals and the locking of the front door had been quite forgotten and might have been lost sight of altogether had not this document turned up in the course of searches for old material.

For the Surveyor of Taxes it was stated that the question here was, whether hotelkeeper, innkeeper, or coffee-house keeper included hydropathic establishment keeper? The Company's action, therefore, put the matter into the category of a test case, of keen interest to all hydropathics in Scotland, of which there were about a dozen at this time, with more being planned.

Here is how *The Glasgow News* of 15th June 1881, reported the Lord President's finding:

The Lord President said that it was conceded that a person carrying on the business of an hotelkeeper in any dwelling-house was liable in respect of the dwelling-house to be charged only at the rate of 6d. in the pound. . . . . . He must carry on the business of an hotelkeeper, and his Lordship supposed he might carry on another business there. Therefore, the circumstance that people in this establishment were—many of them—under medical treatment was in no sense conclusive against the keeper of the establishment carrying on in the building the business of an hotelkeeper. In the next place, it was to be observed that the business of an hotelkeeper was to entertain guests at bed and board, and it was certainly very difficult to say that the appellants did not carry on the business. Every person who came to their house was entertained at bed and board. Some of them got, in addition to that, medical treatment, but that did not prevent them being guests who used the house just as other persons used a hotel—namely to sleep, eat and drink in. But it was said that the rules and regulations of this establishment were such as no hotelkeeper would be allowed to make or carry into effect, and that an hotelkeeper is bound to open his house to all travellers unless there was any special objection to any particular individual; that he was liable for the property of persons in his establishment; and that guests who resort to his house were not liable to have their liberty infringed upon in the manner imposed in this establishment. In the first place, with regard to the obligation of the hotelkeeper to receive all lawful travellers unless there was some special objection, he did not find anything at all inconsistent with that in the rules of this establishment. It was said that the official persons carrying on this business had power to send away those whom they thought unsuitable. That did not appear to his lordship, when properly construed, to bear that the keepers of this establishment were enabled to refuse guests capriciously and maliciously, and every hotelkeeper must have a certain power of selecting his guests, or, perhaps more precisely, of rejecting his guests. He was bound to attend to the health of his guests and the celebrity of his house, and that would lead to his rejecting other guests. Sometimes people in the position of working-men became for a time very rich and extravagant. They had heard tales of navvies drinking all the champagne and eating all the chickens in a neighbourhood, and if any of this kind of people came to a first class hotel he could not imagine that the landlord had not power to reject them as not suited to the class of persons he was accustomed to receive. On that point there was a pretty wide discretion in a hotelkeeper, and he did not think the clause in reference to this establishment was any wider. Then they did not admit liability for the property of their guests; but he should have no hesitation in holding that they were liable. There were several little things as to dining together and other matters; but these were all competent to a hotelkeeper. Next referring to the fines of 1d. imposed for being late at grace, his lordship said these appeared to him to be ludicrous. Whether they were in the practice of exacting them he did not know; but he was very clear on this, that if they were attempted to be exacted and resisted there were no means of enforcing them. Therefore, he thought they were of no importance. On the whole matter he could not see that this company was not carrying on the business of a hotelkeeper, and he thought, therefore, the rate should be reduced.

The other judges concurred.

Many of the older people who have had associations with the Hydro for most of their lives have spoken to me of bygone days and almost all have helped in some way to add to a fascinating picture.

Another vivid description of life in the Establishment has been given me by a resident who prefers to remain anonymous.

"My father and mother met here in 1887. In those days there were long tables down the length of the dining room. When guests departed the gaps were filled by those left moving up. My father arrived, and was set down beside mother. They were married in six months—my father being 35 and my mother 19!! Now, some points told me by her. No smoking in house *or grounds*. Only square dances allowed—Lancers or Quadrilles. Waltzing was considered too intimate. Week day meals were at the same hours as at present but strict punctuality was required. Bells were rung in all the corridors for five minutes before the hour and all had to be seated before they stopped. Anyone late had a collecting box put under their nose and had to put in a contribution. On Sunday we had supper (I can remember that) at 8 p.m.; when we were served with porridge, tea and toast. Then the lights were lowered and we all went in to prayers, after which all retired to bed. On wet days the Bathmen came up, and all the guests had to march round the Recreation Room—not called the Ballroom in those days—in a long crocodile, and then do our physical jerks. We had prayers in the morning and at 9.30 at night. There was a large tank of boiling water put in the hall at 9.45 along with dozens of large mugs. I'm afraid many of these mugs found their way to the bedrooms where something (!) was added to the water.

"Another feature of the Hydro in those days were the picnics which were got up for the guests. They had several large 'wagonettes' holding about 12 people, and they gave us a tea basket, and sticks to make a fire to boil the kettle. We had strict instructions not to set the heather on fire. It took the whole afternoon to go to the Sma' Glen and back. To go to St. Fillans took a whole day and we had sandwiches as well as tea. There was also skating on Ochtertyre Loch and my mother used to speak of those happy days.

"One of the great joys of my youth was croquet, and oh! how

spiteful we were. It was our aim to send our opponent's ball over the bank and away down the avenue!

"There was only one chef in the kitchen; all the rest of the kitchen staff were women who were not allowed upstairs. So all the men on the staff—bathmen, gardeners, joiners, plumbers, porters, etc.—had to take their turn at carving the meat, which was done in the dining room. The maids all had spotless white aprons and large, frilly caps.

"There was no h. and c. in those days and we had large cans of water put at our bedroom doors morning and evening. There was a drinking fountain in the hall, and everyone was told that the water came from a spring which had great curative virtues for all ills. When they were altering the hall on re-opening after 1945 they found a tap on the main supply and so that story was exploded. I saw the remains of the fountain (marble) lying in one of the fields not so long ago!!"

What a marvellous picture! The "crocodile" and physical jerks on wet days, under the eyes of the bathmen. The mugs of boiling water at night. The picnics. The bathmen and joiners and others carving the joints.

This same lady told me that the boys and girls who knew the ropes found a fine hiding place from parents searching for them—the little balcony outside the bedroom floor just above the baths. Parents never thought of looking there.

A curious phrase for a locus for meeting of the young was "on the pigskins". Apparently, at one time about the beginning of the Second World War, in the alcove where the office now is, and which was not then enclosed, there stood a number of couches covered in pigskin. This, it seems, constituted the headquarters of the young bloods of both sexes and came to be rather monopolised by them, just as the right hand corner of the entrance to the ballroom came to be by a later generation.

One of Scotland's most popular story tellers in the early decades of this century was the late J. J. Bell, responsible for the inimitable tales about "Wee Macgreegor". In his last book, *I Remember*, he recalls visits around the year 1880 to a Hydropathic Establishment to which he does not give a place name. Those who know can quickly recognise Strathearn House, both by the regime described and stories told.

He begins by stating the original purpose of all hydropathic establishments—"for persons in search of health through the medium of what used to be called the water cure, which simply meant the patient's going into the water, or the water's going into the patient, or, possibly, as Euclid nearly says, each into each . . ."

The Hydropathic he sketches had retained more of its pristine austerities than any other, the terms were extremely moderate, and organisation, service and comfort (without rank luxury) were mechanically perfect. "The wheels went round, and nothing ever seemed to interrupt their smooth and steady revolution." Mr Bell's own visits never included one in the summer, so he goes on to describe a November visit, arriving early in the evening. At the railway junction, a few miles from their destination, a porter comes along, opening each door and asking "Anyone for the Hydropathic?", so that he can inform the manager of that place of the number of guests coming, "*not*, as a would-be wit once observed, to warn the Establishment to provide an extra egg".

Half an hour later, the guests sign in and, leaving the office, find themselves in a very long, red-carpeted corridor and come presently to a broad, easy staircase, which they ascend—there is no lift yet—to another very long, red-carpeted corridor. To their bedrooms, "which to a reasonable being leave nothing to be desired, except, perhaps, the use of the gas after 10.30 p.m.", comes a maid, evidently chosen for her homely, pleasant exterior, as well as her domestic capability, bringing hot water. They do not put on dinner dress, for the dinner hour is one o'clock, and besides, to do so would result in undesirable excitement for the other guests and embarrassment for themselves.

"But Hark! What are 'those chimes so sweetly stealing'? 'Tis the tocsin for Tea! No harsh and vulgar gong is beaten in these premises."

The house is not full, but the two tables occupied by about 100 guests seem very, very long. At the head of table No. 1 is the doctor's chair, which to-night may or may not be filled by that gentleman. On its right and left are the seats of honour attainable only by the oldest residents; next to them are the places of the second oldest residents; and so on downwards. While this rule of precedence is strictly enforced usually, it may be relaxed; for example, if a husband arrives for the week-end, his wife having been in residence during the previous fortnight.

"Modestly we take our seats at the foot of Table No. 2. We are not making a long stay, so are not tormented by ambition. If we were, we should find our prospects of large advancement none too favourable. There are persons present who will probably remain for months. . . .

"At the head of the room the black and white servitresses stand in a straight, stiff line, motionless, the manager and the head table-maid a pace behind. Among the guests is conversation, but it could not be called a buzz.

"Above the manager, the big, white-faced clock on the wall points silently to six.

"*Ting.*

"The manager has rung the spring-bell. On the assembly falls a hush, solemn, expectant. Half-way down Table No. 1, a reverend gentleman rises and asks a blessing, which may extend to some length, but is usually brief. If there be two reverend gentlemen present, the other will ask a blessing to-morrow, before breakfast. Even were there seven present, there would be no confusion or competition. These things are discreetly arranged by the manager. But, says somebody, supposing no minister is present—what then? Why, then the doctor would officiate, or, in the doctor's absence, the manager himself. There is no record of the head table-maid's asking a blessing."

Tea was then served—a "plain tea", but with plenty of perfectly-made toast, bread and butter, jams and jellies, scones, cookies, biscuits and cakes (not too rich). No pastry. A plain tea for everyone except the new arrivals, who were offered the choice of cold meat or a boiled egg. This was not parsimony, Mr Bell explains; it was simply the method.

"In the year 1880 or thereabouts people did not go to the Hydropathics to be pampered or fed up—in the older sense of the phrase; they expected only simple fare, well cooked and nicely served, and usually they got it. There was no worrying about vitamins then. A fairly substantial breakfast and mid-day dinner, tea with abundance of bread-stuffs—and if you didn't become well and strong, there was something organically wrong with you."

After tea he goes for a smoke in the smoking-room. Smoking is strictly forbidden except in that room, which is placed where the Management do not wish you to find it.

To get there he goes through the entrance hall, out to cross the somewhat gloomy vestibule, and in the corner to the left of the outer doors is a narrow glazed door which opens on a little turret stair. Ascending, feeling chilled, and opening another glazed door, he finds himself in a chamber of depressing dinginess, none too well lit, appointed with a miscellaneous collection of furniture that makes one feel far from home, and a small fire that strives to look hospitable.

"This, sir, is the smoking-room! A few 'devotees of the weed', well-named in the circumstances, come after us, and we all sit down on the least uninviting chairs, and remark, 'What a place!' Some of us are, perhaps, a little more descriptive than that. We then light up and proceed to say what we think of the Management, which is always the main topic of conversation in this room.

"No one, unless he be very unhappily married, remains in the smoking-room after he has finished smoking; and, being satisfied, we betake ourselves to the drawing-room, the abode of virtue. It is a magnificent, many-windowed room, generously carpeted, comfortably furnished, with a small pipe-organ used only at prayers, and a fine grand piano, on which courageous guests occasionally play solos or the accompaniments of equally courageous singers. The music is almost always of a strictly drawing-room quality. Once upon a time an exuberant young doctor, playing his own accompaniment, burst into a dreadful comic song. The general effect would have given Mr H. M. Bateman (cartoonist) inspiration for a masterpiece.

"I cannot remember whether cards were forbidden then; I never saw them. Possibly whist, if played strictly for love, would have been permitted. Still, it was the policy of the Management to avoid anything that might engender severe excitement."

In the recreation room what a scene of gaiety! "The Irresistible Quadrilles" is being played on the piano and eight persons, none older than forty, are gliding through figure 4 of the dance. "This Quadrille business, as many excellent Hydropathists will tell you, is just the thin end of the wedge. In ten years it will be the Polka, and after that the wicked Waltz. What are Hydropathics coming to? Bless their good old-fashioned souls! Well for them that they cannot peep into the future—Hydropathics becoming licensed hotels and subsisting on frivolity!"

"In the broad passage from the Recreation Room to the corridor, so that the passer-by may best distract or disturb the player, stands the billiard table. Yet, after all, distractions and disturbances affect the play but negligibly, for the table itself is so untrue that it would not matter if the cues—some of which might be the better of tips—were twisted, and the balls elliptical (see p. 19).

"Then how, you may reasonably ask, does one, apart from an odd set of Quadrilles, recreate in the Recreation Room? Well, sir, I fear my memory fails in that direction. I know I have seen children sliding on the floor, and heard them being told not to do that; and once I witnessed some young people disporting themselves with battledore and shuttlecock. I seem to have heard of mature people submitting to drill from the bathman, and marching round the room, while avoiding one another's glances as far as possible. It is a fact, however, that concerts have been held in the Recreation Room, and that games involving some bodily activity, such as 'Spin the Plate', have taken place; but these things happened in the busy holiday season. . . . . . If this craving for sportive exercise is not to be overcome by will-force, then I will whisper to you, sir, that somewhere in the bowels of this great building, as I have been credibly informed, is a skittle alley. Like the smoking-room, it is not advertised. Perhaps the Management after its construction realised that skittles suggested beer, and hoped that the alley's existence might be forgotten. My informant, indeed, complained that the game made him feel thirsty, and he was sick-tired of water; moreover, he was limping badly, his opponent having apparently mistaken him for a skittle. . . .

"At a spot which anyone seeking either of the exits must pass, an old lady of placid countenance sits knitting industriously. As you go by, the ball of wool falls from her lap and rolls away.

Being a decent sort of young man, you capture and return it. She thanks you silently with a small sweet smile, and in a sleight of hand fashion gives you a small folded paper. Something tells you not to open it in her presence, but once you get round the corner you examine it. It is not a Five-pound note. It is a Tract. I do not know what yours will be about, but mine was entitled, 'Don't go in, John!' and bore the picture of a man surveying the door of a public house. . . .

"But it grows late—9.30! In the dining-room you will find milk, bread, butter and cheese; in the corridor, on the wall, is a little marble fountain, which on pressing a button, miraculously delivers almost boiling water. Charge your glass, drink up, and have another!

"9.45—and once more the chimes! Prayers in the drawing-room. A minister, failing whom the doctor, officiates. A hymn—a chapter—a prayer—all over in ten minutes. People proceed to say goodnight. The drawing-room empties. The lights sink slowly down in warning—then out.

"We go upstairs. You are not tired, but the bed looks very comfortable. What about finishing that wonderful tale, by Charles Reade, *It's Never too Late to Mend*, which you were reading in the train? Only a couple of chapters left. You make your preparations, get in and adjust the pillows. You open your book, find the place, pick up the thread . . .

"The light goes out."

Many well-known persons from different walks of life, have stayed at the Hydro. Celebrated divines, some of them destined to become Moderators of their Church Assemblies; missionairies whose names are now known throughout the Christian world, like Miss Mary Slessor, of Calabar, came to the Hydro. She arrived once, bringing two sets of black twins from Africa. (In those days twin babies born to women in some African tribes were killed off.) The "Tartan Pimpernel"—the Rev. Dr Donald Caskie—came in recent days.

The Frys of Bristol, the Rowntrees of York; William Booth, before he became General Booth of the Salvation Army; and Dr Benson, who later became Archbishop of Canterbury all stayed here; also Mr Quarrier who set up the orphan homes at Bridge of Weir, Renfrewshire; the Scottish novelist, 'Ian Maclaren' (the Rev. Dr John Watson), and many others, according to James Caw, whose book, *Reminiscences of Forty Years on the Staff of a Hydro*, tells numerous amusing stories of the House in its early days.

Douglas McLennan, formerly head porter, tells me that he has seen five millionaires in the Winter Garden at one time.

Amongst the laymen living in the Hydro at the time of the 1871 Census was Alexander Stephen, aged 39, master shipbuilder, accompanied by his wife, two sons and two daughters, and his mother. He belonged to the family who have built up the famous business of Alexander Stephen's of Linthouse, Glasgow, whither the firm had just moved, and Frederick John Stephen, then aged seven and staying with his father in Strathearn House, later became chairman of the company and also one of the Clyde's great international yachtsmen.

One man who gave me at first hand some of his impressions of Strathearn House was the late Lord Kirkwood, better known simply as Davie Kirkwood, M.P.

Shortly after the Second World War, while working in London, I was asked to write an article based on reminiscences of "Red Clydeside" by David Kirkwood, who became the Member of Parliament for Dumbarton and Clydebank Burghs. He had been one of the original Red Clydesiders, so who better to talk on this subject than he?

"Because o' the trouble at Beardmore's works in Glasgow, they 'deportit me'."

"Deported you?" I said, in horror, thinking of the slave labour of 150 years ago.

"Aye, deportit me to Edinburgh."

Apparently he was sent to Edinburgh and had to report at the Castle once or twice a week, being restricted to an area of five miles radius from the Castle. That was no deterrent and he enjoyed many pleasant walks through the Pentland Hills. In January 1917, he went off to the Labour Party Conference in Manchester and when it was over Kirkwood went home to Glasgow instead of reporting back to Edinburgh Castle. Early next morning two plain-clothes detectives knocked him up and asked him to come along with them. He refused, saying that he was going back to bed and if they came back later in the day he'd go with them. No one came for him, so three days later his friends took him to Crieff Hydro for a rest. There he had a pleasant time.

"The place was fu' o' ministers," he went on. "An' d'ye know this? They were playin' cards all evenin'. I thought that was terrible." He gave a wry smile and added, softly, "An' me a revolutionary."

While at the Hydro he attended the morning services in the drawing room and enjoyed them; "especially the lassie playing the organ after the service". It was while he was sitting there, lost in the music, that one of the porters found him and said he was wanted in the Manager's office. When he got there two soldiers awaited him, to take him back to Edinburgh. When he went up to the third floor to get his things the soldiers accompanied him and he pointed out to them the lovely view, south and west, and told them—one of them astonished at his *sang-froid* in the face of a return to prison—the names of the hills and the different counties they could see.

That, so far as I can find, is the only record of an arrest taking place in the Hydro!

It must be added that long before the Directors knew about the strictures passed on the billiard tables and the balls (p.16), they had had the tables re-covered and made sure that the balls were spherical.

FOUNDER OF THE FELLOWSHIP

"The rank is but the guinea's stamp,
The man's the gowd for a' that".

BURNS

Who were the men who built this business so that it grew and prospered until now, at the opening of its second century, Strathearn Hydropathic Establishment marches on, full of vigour, full of ideas that give the onlooker a feeling of the joys of youth?

Credit is due to many men throughout the decades, but they themselves would be the first to admit that one man alone bears the palm. Like Atlas with the world on his shoulders, this man bore the shocks and basked in the sunshine with equanimity; moulded circumstances to his will; solved innumerable problems of protocol, and produced a fellowship out of a floating, changing kaleidoscope of characters, male and female.

That man was, of course, Thomas Henry Meikle; Doctor Meikle as he was known to all connected with the Hydro from its inception until his death in 1913.

One cannot say that he was typical of his colleagues, the directors of the Establishment, for he was not an ordinary man, but he had traits that were common to most of those others; they were all God-fearing and, if we may judge by their actions as shown in the minutes of their meetings, kindly men. Shrewd men, too, as the record of the Company shows, and prepared to stand up for their rights.

They were strict and believed in discipline; not just discipline for others, but self-discipline, that sneered-at and neglected quality of our own times.

Smoking and the drinking of alcoholic beverages were forbidden in the House when it opened and no reference to the latter appears anywhere in the minutes until the year 1949, when an application to the Perthshire Licensing Court for a licence to sell liquor with meals was refused.

PLATE I

Dr. Thomas Henry Meikle

PLATE 2

The Hydro from the North

Needless to say, some of the visitors to the Hydro did not take kindly to the "No Smoking" rule. The first minute book of the directors' meetings tells that on 12th October, 1869, they received

"... a deputation consisting of Major Thomson and Mr Wilson. On behalf of themselves and others in the Establishment they requested some relaxation of the rule which prohibited smoking within the Company's premises. The Directors, after respectfully considering the request agreed that it was not expedient to make any change in the rule."

As a protest against this rule, smokers indulged their vice sitting on the wall of the grounds.

Almost exactly four years later a minute stated:

"A smoking room having been continually called for by many of the visitors, the meeting, though still of the same opinion, adverse to making any provision for this baneful practice, yet in the circumstances, on the ground of expediency, agreed to authorise a bath room in the tower to be converted to that use."

Fifty-four years later—November 1926—it was decided that cigarettes and matches should be kept for sale by the Billiard Marker. So ended that "strange, eventful history", a measure to some extent of the kind of men the Directors were. At the same time it should be remembered that for the first forty years the Hydropathic lived up to its name and received almost as many patients requiring hydrotherapeutic treatment as those who came for rest and recreation. The function of the Establishment was never lost sight of even when water cure facilities were bereft of their first, strong appeal.

How heavily and securely the directors leaned on Dr Meikle! Time and again in the old minute book, notes like the following appear:

"The Manager (Dr Meikle) said he had a plan to enlarge the kitchen and improve the ventilation 'felt to be so injurious in the busy season'. It was left to him to do this as economically as possible." (1879)

"Directors approved of the Chairman's (Dr. Meikle) arrangements for securing a five years lease of Dryton Park, on Ferntower Estate at a rent of £23."

That was in April 1902, and in the same minutes a decision
as to employing a band of musicians was left to the Chairman;
also whether to employ a "lady housekeeper" from Peebles
Hydro. Dryton Park is one of the farms now owned by
the Hydropathic Company.

So it went on. Yet in the midst of his multifarious duties
the Doctor found time to take part in public affairs and to
indulge his benevolent nature in giving, both privately and
publicly. It was he who presented the Knock of Crieff to
the town. It was he who, when the Royal Hotel came up for
sale paid almost £4,000 for it and gave it to the townspeople
as the Strathearn Institute, still in use to this day. He was a
town councillor, Chairman of the Gas Company, Honorary
president of the Y.M.C.A., and took an active interest in
politics.

Born in the Border parish of Lilliesleaf, near Melrose,
Roxburghshire, on 24th May 1834, Thomas Henry Meikle
was the second son of Thomas Meikle and Helen Hannay or
Meikle. At that time his father was factor to Mr Sprot of
Riddell, one of the most ancient of Border families. His
mother came from Wigtownshire where her father farmed
Baldoon Mains, in the parish of Kirkinner, a mile or two
south of the county town. Her marriage proclamation is in
the old parish register for 15th April 1831. Their first
child was William, born in May, 1832.

Of Thomas's childhood nothing is known, and only
conjecture and reconstruction bring us a little of his
adolescence, which is closely bound up with the activities of
his older brother. William, after his schooling, went to
study at the University of Edinburgh, graduated Doctor of
Medicine there in 1857, and immediately travelled north to
Aberdeen to assist Dr Alexander Munro with the running of
Loch-Head Hydropathic, situated about a mile to the
north-east of the centre of the city.

His sister Margaret Helen, had gone to Loch-Head a

year or two before William graduated, but whether to work or for treatment we do not know. We do know, however, that she died there on 18th June 1856, aged 20. Dr Munro had attended her and William Meikle signed the death certificate. Their father, when he retired, a year or two later, also went to live at Loch-Head, and died there in 1860.

In the meantime Thomas began his studies at Aberdeen University, for the home at Riddell ceased to exist after the death there of Aunt Eliza Meikle in 1856. She had kept house for them since their mother's death in 1840, on the arrival of Peter, the youngest of the family. The national census of 1841 gives the following names and ages of the household: Thomas (45), Elizabeth (50), sister and house-keeper; William (9), Thomas Henry (7), Margaret (5), James (3), and Peter (eight months).

Very soon after going to Loch-Head in 1857, Dr William Meikle bought the establishment, but his happy planning for the future with his wife and family was doomed never to reach fruition, for he died there on 26th November 1858. William's wife, before her marriage, was Eliza Hannay, born in Penninghame parish in Wigtownshire, and I think it probable that she was related to William's mother. Thomas Meikle senior, like Margaret and William before him, was buried at Riddell.

In 1864 Eliza Meikle married again. Her husband was the Rev. Dr Joseph Leckie of Millport, on the Great Cumbrae, in the Firth of Clyde, and, from 1866, of Ibrox, Glasgow.

On forming the Company to operate the Hydropathic Establishment, in 1867, Dr Meikle did not forget his sister-in-law, for her name as Mrs Leckie, in the first list of share-holders, forms the original link between the Leckie family and the Hydro. She was the great-grandmother of Mr John Leckie, the present manager.

This is an era in the story of the Meikle family which has made the biographer long in vain for a miracle—a dusty packet of old letters, a diary, found hidden in some attic, revealing a hundred interesting details of the intimate life of the individuals and families being studied, and answering such questions as: How Thomas came to meet and marry

Margaret Ballingall Paterson, whose father, James Paterson, farmed from Melness House, close to the village of that name in the County of Sutherland? How the romance progressed? How, having fixed the wedding day for 20th August 1861, just a few months after he graduated Doctor of Medicine at Aberdeen, he transported himself and some of his family to Melness, a tiny township on the north coast of Scotland? Not one of those intriguing points is known.

Once safely back at Loch-Head the young couple would settle down and Thomas's working life would begin to take shape. "The establishment at Loch-Head was conducted in a quiet, home-like way, and was a favourite resort of ministers." So says a book on hydropathy, written some 60 years ago.

A quiet life, however, was not Thomas Meikle's idea of living, and within a few years he began his quest for something bigger and better. Here, once more, we must fall back on vague phrases like the one from many of the prospectuses:

"This Establishment occupies a most advantageous site in a district of great natural and historical interest, selected by Dr Meikle from many others in Scotland . . ."

A search throughout Scotland for a suitable site; the sounding out of men of substance for their financial support in a new venture of some magnitude—these were not achievements of a moment's duration, and from Crieff's "early warning system"—the local newspaper—it is known that the straws in the wind were blowing Crieff-wise by 1865. In February 1866, as much as a year before any formal meeting to form a company to finance the project was held, the *Strathearn Herald* came away with a paragraph to the effect that a hydropathic establishment seemed likely to be erected in Crieff, and all through that year the newspaper continued to print scraps of information in connection with the proposed hydropathic. Some of these paragraphs are to be found in the chapter below dealing with the erection and development of the establishment itself.

From all this it may safely be assumed that Thomas Meikle was working on his scheme for a big hydro in 1865 and possibly even earlier. No doubts ever seemed to linger in—indeed, ever seemed to *enter*—his mind that he would not raise the capital needed for such a venture; or that he would not make a success of it when it came into being.

His experience at Loch-Head, combined with his extraordinary long-sightedness, made him speedily realise the possibilities of the hydropathic system of treating invalids, and he almost certainly read voraciously everything published about the water cure. He even wrote a small treatise on hydrotherapeutics. The sense of being cared for and cosseted is very dear to all of us, while apparent freedom of action, behind which lay concealed a certain gentle discipline, as in the matters of rising in time for breakfast, going to bed, "lights out", turning up promptly for meals, no smoking or drinking (except water), gave the guests a fillip in being made to do things which they would not have thought of doing or been perhaps permitted to do in their own spheres.

In the course of his search for his ideal site Dr Meikle remembered his friend of long standing, Hew Miller, who had been working for over ten years on the Ochtertyre Estate, near Crieff, and, as Crieff was by this time a known resort of holiday-makers, it seemed worth while going to have a look at the place.

In such simple ways are our destinies shaped. For here was the field of $15\frac{1}{2}$ acres, called Galvelbeg, on the south-west shoulder of the Knock, available to feu, exactly where the Hydropathic stands to-day.

While he was seeking a site, which he eventually found in Crieff, for a Hydropathic, Dr Meikle's wife had borne him daughters and a son, and life generally tasted very good. Only a matter of ten weeks after his 34th birthday the Strathearn Hydropathic Establishment opened its doors— *and he was in complete command.*

For the next 25 years he remained in that position and from time to time undertook additional responsibilities. In May 1896, he succeeded his cousin, Wm. Meikle actuary of Glasgow Savings Bank, and founder of the Meikle Trust, as Chairman and retained that office till his death. The

Strathearn Herald after his death on 4th March 1913, details some of the facts about his younger days and the development of the Hydropathic Establishment, and goes on:

In private life Dr Meikle was of a kindly and sympathetic nature and not only his numerous staff of servants but many others in humble station, whom he chanced to come in contact with, have had occasion to bless his generous hand, which was frequently engaged in that quiet, unostentatious manner of giving that is all the more appreciated because it is not widely known.

A staunch Churchman, he was, since ever he came to Crieff, an attached member of the United Presbyterian (now St. Andrew's) Church, and was one of its oldest elders. But his deep and practical interest in religious matters was by no means confined to the denomination with which he was immediately associated. All Christian work had his keen sympathy and hearty support, and he devised several schemes whereby those actively engaged in Church work might enjoy the health-giving facilities offered by the Strathearn Hydropathic to its more wealthy patrons . . . He took a prominent part in the Church Union negotiations of 1900, and prior to his recent serious illness he evinced a deep interest in the present wider Union proposals.

He was one of the County J.P.s and took a warm interest in the Temperance Cause . . . For several years he was a member of Crieff Town Council. The local Gas Company also found in him a wise and efficient chairman for a long number of years. In the realm of politics he was an ardent Liberal prior to the Gladstonian split over Irish Home Rule in 1886, when he became a Liberal Unionist . . . and an honorary president of the Crieff Unionist Association.

Dr Meikle was twice married, his second wife, who survives him, being a daughter of the late David Paton, of the well-known Alloa firm of woollen manufacturers. He is also survived by a family of four daughters and one son by the former marriage, the latter being Dr T. Gordon Meikle, the present resident physician in Strathearn Hydropathic and who has been for many years assistant to his father in the management of the Establishment.

The funeral was private, those attending including relatives, a few intimate friends and the heads of departments in the Hydropathic—Messrs. Caw, Stenhouse, Reid, Calazel

and others.   One of the ten carriages had to be used solely
for wreaths.

In the 'Seventies and 'Eigthies of last century, before
Mrs Margaret Meikle died on 22nd June 1883, at Strathearn
Leigh, the family consisted of seven children—Margaret
Helen (18), Thomas Gordon (17), Bessie MacKay (15),
Marjorie Jane (14), Sarah Ann (11), Edith Patricia (7), and
James Reay (5).   The four oldest were all born at Loch-
Head, Aberdeen, and the ages given are from the census of
1881.

That same census has an interesting note, following the
list of the family, for it includes as a visitor, staying with
the Meikles, Joseph Hannay Leckie, aged 15; the same
Joseph Leckie who became a director of the Company in
1910.   The names of 46 persons staying in the Hydro at the
time of the census come under the title, "Boarders", and they
were being looked after by 34 servants.   The census was
taken early in April, so the numbers were not high.   Ten
years previously there were 84 guests and 30 servants in the
House at the census time.

The fact that young Leckie visited the Meikles in this
way shows that the Doctor had not lost touch with his
brother's widow.   When, 29 years later, Dr Meikle suggested that the Board should appoint Joseph Leckie a
Director, he introduced him as his "brother-in-law"—a slip
of the tongue on the Doctor's part.   Incidentally, he was the
first of the name Leckie to attend meetings of the Company
and take an active interest in it.

There are periodic mentions in the minute books of shares
being transferred from Dr Meikle to his family, but, as time
goes by some of the names drop out and, by the end of the
First World War we are left with four—Marjorie, Bessie,
Edith and, of course, Dr T. Gordon Meikle; Dr Gordon
as he was called to distinguish him from his famous father.

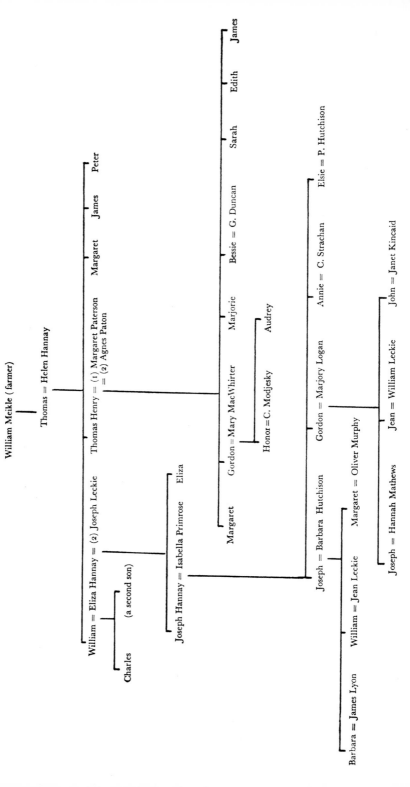

CRIEFF AND THE HYDROPATHIC

"The habitable globe possesses no more
delightful spot than Crieff."

Charles Reade

Strathearn Herald—24 March 1866

Hydropathic Establishment—It gives us great pleasure to hear that there is some prospect of an institution of this kind being erected in Crieff. We understand that Dr Meikle, of Loch-Head Hydropathic Establishment, Aberdeen, was here this week, looking after a suitable site, and, we believe, that if a sufficient supply of water be got, the site, fixed upon, which is a most admirable one, is likely to be had on most advantageous terms. We need not tell our Crieff friends that, in the erection of such a beneficial establishment, they would secure an institution that would go far to place Crieff in a position of prosperity that it has never yet attained to.

This prophetic note, besides showing the shrewdness of David Philips, editor and owner of the *Strathearn Herald*, in assessing the future worth of the Hydropathic to the town, also emphasises the perspicacity of Dr Thomas Henry Meikle, the founder of Strathearn Hydropathic and the amount of time and thought he had given to such a project.

It poses, too, several pertinent questions. What qualities had Crieff to give it preference over any one of a dozen other places in Scotland? Was it weather, a matter on which Dr Meikle consulted Alexander Buchan, the author of the "cold spells"? How did Dr Meikle come to Crieff and decide to build a hydropathic there?

Why Crieff?

"The natural advantages of the town are of a high order—a healthy, bracing atmosphere, calculated to restore the invalid, and to preserve the vigour of the robust. Plenty of water power. The water with which the town is supplied being almost unrivalled for sparkling purity; the beautiful, romantic neighbourhood studded with mansions and castles surrounded with classic grounds. Were these natural facilities turned to account, Crieff

might become in one generation the most coveted summer
retreat in Scotland perhaps. But a proper local government has
not yet been constituted. No regular provision has yet been
made for paving and lighting the streets. Our streets are not yet
honored with written names, nor are our houses numbered. Yet
the people are shrewd, and have borne themselves well in peace
and war."

That is a quotation from *Rambles Round Crieff* by Sinclair
Korner, Ph.D., published in 1858, ten years before the
Hydropathic opened, and one phrase there should be
particularly noted, for it is repeated in other books and
articles written about that period. "The water with which
the town is supplied being almost unrivalled for sparkling
purity." The streets are now well lit, but the paving,
especially of side-walks, may even now leave something to be
desired.

Thomas Meikle came to Crieff to look around and to
examine the possibility of building a hydropathic there.

It was a great stroke of fortune when he was shown the
field called Galvelbeg, halfway up the Knock, and over-
looking a great portion of lovely Strathearn.

There it was—a perfect site for a fine building, offered to
him by the Ochtertyre Estate on generous terms. This site,
exactly where the Hydropathic stands to this day, was at that
period an "island", surrounded by the lands of the powerful
Drummond family—Lady Willoughby d'Eresby (*née* Drummond), of Drummond Castle—and the lands of Mr
Anthony Murray of Dollerie. It is not difficult to imagine
Thomas Meikle's feelings in that hour—his dreams coming
true; a stately edifice, sheltered from the harsh north winds
by the pine-clad Knock; open to the southern sun and the
little hills and great mountains of the west; confident, and
yet tremulous in the first flush of realisation of his enormous
good luck and the prospects lying hidden among the future
years.

A glance at an old wood-cut of the hamlet of Crieff as it
was in 1854 shows a scattered little place, entered by crossing
a bridge with several arches, over the River Earn. This is
the old bridge—the present one was built at almost the same

time as the Hydropathic—but it has the same awkward turn as there is to-day for the traveller approaching from the south, though it was easily negotiable by horse traffic. It was narrow, too, and vehicles could not pass one another on it. At that time much of the town was situated around the south end of the bridge, even to the extent of a factory with a chimney stack. This was known as Bridge End to distinguish it from the—perhaps—more select part on higher ground. Bridge End once claimed the right to be recognised as a separate entity and not a part of Crieff, and insisted rather riotously on having its own Provost and Town Council, and there was also the village of Drummond which became the eastern part of the amalgam—the town of Crieff.

The meaning of the word, Crieff, is variously given as derived from the Gaelic *Crubha*, a haunch. (The 'bh' sounds 'v' in Gaelic.) This is thought to refer to the Knock of Crieff. Other offerings as to the derivation are:—*Craobh*, a tree, from which, again, you get *Craoibh*, among the trees.

The town is very old though the earliest mention is apparently the year 1218, and in 1681 it was described in a charter by Charles II as *"Burgum de Crieff, Burgum Capitale Senescallatus de Strathearn"*—the Capital of the Steward of Strathearn. Next to Perth, Crieff was the principal town in the county. The Earls Palatine of Strathearn, with their wide, regal powers of jurisdiction, exercised almost certainly at the Skait of Crieff,* disappeared towards the end of the fifteenth century, and to some extent Crieff's importance waned for a time. In a charter dated 1688 there is a clause erecting a part of Crieff, called Pittenzie or Galvelmore, into the Burgh of Regality of Drummond.

Any good road map of Scotland will disclose the secret of Crieff's rise to fame, which began in the last decades of the seventeenth century and went on until around 1770, as one of the most notable cattle markets in Britain. Roads from north, west, east and south converge on the town, where,

---

* The Skait of Crieff lay about half a mile south of the town, and it seems to have been a mound adapted for the purpose of a meeting place—12 yards in diameter and enclosed by a low turf wall. In mediaeval times Courts of Justice were invariably held in the open.

in the second week of October each autumn, 30,000 "black" cattle were brought for sale. Buyers came from all over England as well as the Lowlands of Scotland, and large sums of money—about 30,000 guineas—changed hands. Indeed, in A. R. B. Haldane's intensely interesting book, *The Drove Roads of Scotland*, he states that Crieff at the end of the seventeenth century "became the greatest cattle market in Scotland, a position which it retained for well over half a century . . . Much of the trade was done by means of bills, and during the second quarter of the eighteenth century Crieff came to be regarded as one of the main financial centres of Scotland. Considerable sums, however, also changed hands in the form of gold as MacKy has described, and an entry in the Minute Book of the Royal Bank of Scotland in 1730 shows that tellers were that year sent from Edinburgh to Crieff with £3,000 in notes to put into circulation in return for cash."

These annual Trysts at Crieff lasted for about a week, but fairs had been held at various points throughout the country from towards the end of the sixteenth century, as shown by authentic records, and they were the most important commercial and economic events of the year to a large section of the populace.

As may well be imagined, the wild men of the north and west struck terror into the hearts of the douce people of the countryside around Crieff, and although the Earl of Perth, who had been empowered by Act of Parliament in 1672 to hold "ane yeirlie fair and weiklie mercat", also held a court to regulate disputes and keep order, the Highlanders forcibly billeted themselves on householders in the country round about, breaking in if need be for that purpose, and often carrying off some of the household goods. Yet towards the end of the eighteenth century the old folk were speaking with great regret of the passing of the Trysts.

"Tryst" is a Scots word, possibly from the word trust, and it came to mean an agreed meeting place between buyers and sellers, for the cattle dealers "trysted" the owners of the beasts to meet at a certain place on a certain date.

When Falkirk replaced Crieff in the favour of the dealers

and the drovers, in the second half of the eighteenth century, Crieff's second phase of importance passed. After all the years during which the summer months were spent anticipating the Tryst, and the winter months in regretting it, the town and surrounding countryside settled into a quiet somnolence, disturbed but not broken by the arrival each year at the time of the erstwhile Trysts, of the Earl of Perth's men to police the market. These were certain of his feuars whose charters bound them to act as guards during the period of the Tryst, and the second statistical Account of Scotland, published in 1845, states that those services had not long ceased to be exacted, though the Trysts had vanished 75 years earlier. It should be said here, that the Earl of Perth was not a disinterested person in the matter of the markets, for he was entitled to collect a fee of twopence per animal, but, says Haldane, "the right of collecting these was let by him for a yearly sum of £600 Scots (£50 sterling) to a tenant who made what he could on the transaction".

To turn for a moment to the fortunes of Crieff during times of war, it seems that the people of the town were almost always supporting the monarch who was on the throne. The Marquis of Montrose, fighting to restore Charles I to the throne, took up a strong position on Callum's Hill, in 1664, and spent a winter there. The townspeople were friendly—they could hardly be aught else—but they suffered sadly for their loyalty to the reigning monarch when the Chevalier (son of James VII and proclaimed James VIII on the Braes of Mar on 6th September 1715) came to reclaim the throne and brought civil war with him. In January of the next year, 350 Highlanders occupied the town, to the great alarm of the inhabitants, who at once set about seeking influential friends to prevent them suffering the fate of Auchterarder and Blackford, both of which had been burned down. They were assured by Drummond of Wester Feddall that no such design was intended, but he played them false, and the town was utterly devastated, every house, it is said, being burned to the ground, and the people left to fend for themselves as best they could in bitter, winter weather.

With the Young Pretender, Charles Edward Stuart, in 1745, came threats of a repeat performance, but through the good offices of the Duke of Perth, Laird of Drummond, the town escaped. In fact, the Prince spent a night in Ferntower House as he retreated north in 1746.

The Trysts at Crieff had not been greatly affected by the Risings, and drovers were allowed to carry arms, having been exempted from the Disarming Acts of 1716 and 1748. Those in authority realised that the drovers required gun, sword and pistol—the weapons allowed—as cattle stealing and raiding were still quite common.

So the years passed. Life in the town and district became more and more leisurely, with less and less happening, so that far more folk died in their beds.

Gradually a pattern crept into the yearly round, and with the arrival of the railway in March 1856, greater numbers of visitors began to frequent the district in summer; for the climate was found to be dry and invigorating and the Strath of the Earn full of pleasant walks, while, for the more wealthy, drives to Loch Earn and north through the Sma' Glen proved very popular.

For many years the chief industry in Crieff had been weaving, and six or eight years before the '45, the same Duke of Perth mentioned above established a large linen factory. Alas! the Duke was attainted for his part in the Rising, and the garrison in Crieff, despite the loyalty of the townspeople, destroyed the mill in 1746, and it was never rebuilt. Six years later the Duke's estate came under the control of commissioners who assisted the farmers, gave feus at low rates, established industries such as tanning and paper-making, paid indenture fees for apprentices to different trades, and even presented to the town a bleaching green. Old records show that by 1828 there were three malt distilleries and eight malting houses within the town, but this boom in manufacture did not last, and, apart from weaving and tanning, the little burgh settled back into a quieter era.

When the Hydropathic was built the principal industries in the town included weaving, dyeing, woollen mills, but only one distillery. To-day, the Hydro is the largest employer of labour in the district, and there are new industries such as the numerous garages and agricultural engineering workshops, and the new Strathearn Glass Works, opened in 1965 by Sir Alec Douglas-Home, Member of Parliament for the constituency. Other businesses in the neighbourhood which depend on Crieff for labour are McAinsh's flooring factory and the Dalchonzie mink farm.

An interesting feature on the fringes of the little town at the beginning of last century, was "The Pecks". These were small plots of land on the outskirts of the village and could be rented by householders from the owners of the three estates—Broich, Dollerie and Drummond. According to Porteous' *History of Crieff*, the principal ones were where Broich Terrace is now, and they extended quite a distance down towards the river. Potatoes, kale and oats were the main crops taken off the Pecks.

As the years passed on, Crieff became noted as a health and holiday resort, the Hydro playing a big part in popularising it.

The direct link between Crieff and Perth before 1866 was by stage coach, of which several ran daily, including the Glasgow–Perth and Edinburgh–Perth mail coaches. This form of conveyance had operated through the century and continued to do so after the permanent way reached Crieff from Gleneagles; for the journey to that point and then on to Perth proved tedious and roundabout, but the coaches disappeared once the track from Perth to Crieff via Methven Junction was opened. Going to Glasgow by one of the coaches one travelled by road to Wyndford, near Stirling, where the journey became a voyage, for a switch over to a canal boat took place there.

The railway to Comrie began operations in 1893, 29 years after a company was formed to build it. Later it was extended to Lochearnhead, but the metals have been lifted and the bridges destroyed.

To-day the railway to Crieff is a relic of the past, despite representations by several bodies, including the Hydropathic

Company, for whom the spokesman was Sir Malcolm Knox, one of the Directors.

Crieff now is known as an excellent motoring centre. Braemar and Balmoral may be visited in a day's run, as also may Oban, Fort William and the Great Glen, Glasgow and Edinburgh. In fact, Edinburgh may now be done between luncheon and dinner, going via Glen Devon and the Forth road bridge. Shorter tours include the Trossachs, Loch Tay, Loch Rannoch, Dundee and the Angus coast north of that city, and St. Andrews, via the new Tay road bridge.

PLATE 3

The New Swimming Pool

The Hydro Golf Course

PLATE 4

Board of Directors 1986

Back Row—R. Simpson, G. R. Donaldson, G. T. Ross.
Front Row—R. G. Mickel, G. N. Donaldson *(Chairman)*, W. G. J. Leckie.

STRUGGLES OF THE EARLY DAYS

"...... far-off things,
And battles long ago. ...."

WORDSWORTH

"When was the Hydro built? Was it always a hydropathic, or was it a country house or something like that before it was a hydro?"

Inevitably those two questions are asked when any discussion takes place on the actual structure. The answers are quite straightforward. Strathearn House was planned and erected as a hydropathic. Building began in the late spring of 1867 and the first 40 bedrooms were occupied on 7th August 1868—the opening date, though there was, in fact, no ceremony to mark the occasion.

The architect was Robert Ewan, Aberdeen, and later of Glasgow, and the planner was, of course, Dr Thomas Henry Meikle. Having had charge of Loch-Head Hydropathic in Aberdeen, Dr Meikle knew the lay-out to strive for, the snags to avoid, and as the son of an estate factor he must have known something about buildings and land.

Needless to say, the siting of such an attractive and large establishment on the fringe of the town of Crieff caused great excitement and interest, feelings which even the children enjoyed. A letter I received some time ago said that the writer had often heard Miss Thom, daughter of Dr Alexander Thom who was one of the first Town Commissioners and a medical practitioner, talk about the times her nurse took her for a walk up to Galvelbeg and she and other children played among the piles of sand and stones beside the new building.

The deep interest in the Hydropathic Establishment of the people of Crieff re-echoed through the pages of the *Strathearn Herald* which had been in existence for some ten years before the first news of Dr Meikle's project appeared in its columns. On the 24th February 1866, a year before the provisional directors were arguing in the Cockburn Hotel in Edinburgh about its constitution, a paragraph appeared stating that Crieff was probably to have a hydropathic, and just a month later came this:

We are given to understand that it is almost settled that this establishment will be on in Crieff.

And a fortnight later:

The water from the Barvic.—The bringing of water from the Barvic to supply the proposed Hydropathic Establishment is a matter of great importance to Crieff, more ways than one. The supply that could be got from that stream is likely to be far more than is necessary to serve that establishment, and therefore it becomes a question worthy of great consideration, if it would not be advisable for the town of Crieff to enter into arrangements with the promoters of the Hydropathic Establishment, if that can be done, and by bearing a share of the expense of bringing the water to the front of the Knock, get a supply to the town of Crieff. At the present time when the drainage of the town has been spoken of more times than one, and when the want of water in the houses have been felt to be a great want, this subject is surely worthy of consideration, more especially as no opportunity could turn up so easily to secure the town a supply of water at so cheap a rate. We are aware others are ready to take great advantage of it, and in such a way that, if they succeed, it will bar out a great portion of the town from participating in its benefits. Why has not the Council taken up the matter?

Both the *Herald* and the *Perthshire Advertiser* in December 1866, carried paragraphs about the shares of the Company being bought up, which indicates that Dr Meikle had been busy. The *Advertiser* stated:

Crieff.—The Hydropathic Establishment.—We are glad in being able to state that the whole capital (£20,000) of the proposed hydropathic establishment has been subscribed. The undertaking, it is expected, will be proceeded with early in the ensuing spring. The promoters of the scheme are sanguine of success, from the fact that the salubrity of the climate, combined with the unrivalled scenery of the district, and the recommendations given by several eminent chemists of the quality of the water, which is to be used in the establishment, besides other circumstances, point to the undertaking being a paying concern to the shareholders, and which will ultimately tend to help forward the rapidly growing importance of the district.

That same month (Dec. 1866) the ground was being staked out, according to the *Herald*, but the same procedure is again recorded the following May, and again in June.

In the midst of the other news, including paragraphs about Hydro contracts, there is the refreshing information that William Cullen Bryant, "the father of American poetry", was visiting Crieff. He obviously enjoyed his stay, for he wrote, "I can conscientiously recommend a sojourn in this delightful region"; and "From the Knock you have one of the noblest views in Great Britain."

Before building began, however, the directors had had some dusty meetings to thrash out initial problems. Here are the notes—they can hardly be called minutes—of these meetings, just as they appear in the opening pages of the earliest minute book.

"The first Meeting of the 'Strathearn Sanatorium Company Limited' Provisional Directors was held in the Cockburn Hotel, Edinburgh on 1st February 1867. Present, Mr William Brown, provost of Crieff (in the chair)—Mr Thomas Brown, Elibank, Galashiels, Mr Lambert Barron, advocate, Aberdeen, Dr George Cowan, Edinburgh, Mr Alexr. Collie, Murlingden, Glasgow, Mr James Millar, Dumbarton, Mr David Paton, Alloa, Mr George Rough, Dundee,—Thos H. Meikle, and D. H. Kennedy.

"After a somewhat heated discussion, over the question of Mr Kennedy being named in the Articles of Association as resident Secretary at £100 a year, several of the Directors, especially Mr Paton, objected to this—On this Mr Kennedy resigned all connection with the Company, and induced Mr Barron and Dr Cowan to resign. Mr Millar also resigned but not for the same reason—and before the next meeting Provost Brown had an attack of '*appoplexy*' and was disabled.

"Another meeting of the Provisional Directors was held in the Cockburn Hotel, Edinburgh on 27 Feb. 1867—Mr Rough in the Chair. Having met they again heard Mr Kennedy who still adheres to his resolution and in the circumstances they agree to allow Dr Meikle opportunity to make such arrangements with the shareholders as he may find necessary for carrying on the Company instead of now intimating to the shareholders that they will receive their deposits. After a good deal of Difficulty a new prospectus with a new list of Directors was issued and called the 'Strathearn Hydropathic Establishment Co. Limited' with the following as Provisional Directors:

Charles W. Anderson, Esq., Merchant, Leith.
*William Brown, Esq., Banker, Provost of Crieff.
*Thomas Brown, Esq., Elibank, Galashiels.
Andrew Buchan, Esq., Tweedgreen, Peebles.
*Alexander Collie, Esq., of Murlingden, Glasgow.
John MacLeish, Esq., Banker, Crieff.
William Meikle, Esq., Banker, Glasgow.
*David Paton, Esq., Manufacturer, Tillicoultry.
John Pullar, Esq., St. Leonard's Bank, Perth.
*George Rough, Esq., Osborne Place, Dundee.

those marked with an * being in the original lists. The Company were registered on 23rd April 1867—and the first meeting thereafter held in Glasgow on 2nd May 1867."

The first prospectus, issued in February 1867, showed the title of the Company to be Strathearn Sanatorium Company, Limited, and the Capital to be £21,000 in shares of £25 each. The provisional Directors were as given in the first paragraph of the above notes except for one additional name; that of Walter Thorburn, banker, Peebles. Thomas Henry Meikle was named as Physician and D. H. Kennedy, advocate, Aberdeen, as Secretary.

In the following month a second prospectus came out for Strathearn Hydropathic Establishment Company, Limited with the Directors as given in the second list. No secretary was named, and the law agents were J. & J. Boyd, writers, Glasgow.

Somewhere about the end of May or early June a third prospectus was issued, with no changes in the personnel, but Dr Meikle was described as "Physician and Manager". He had already been appointed interim secretary—an "interim" that was to stretch through the years until 1892, when Dr Meikle's son, Dr Gordon Meikle was appointed to assist his father "in the various duties of his office".

Although this third prospectus described Dr Meikle as

the "Physician and Manager", the second prospectus is much the most interesting, for it indicates not only terms to be charged but also estimates of the cost of running the Hydropathic and the cost of building it.

The most noteworthy paragraphs are these:

An arrangement has been made with Dr Thomas H. Meikle by which he agrees to transfer to the Company the good-will of the business which has been successfully carried on at Loch-Head for the last sixteen years, and to give his own services as Medical Superintendent.

It is intended that the Establishment shall be of the very best description. The Baths shall combine every appliance which experience has proved to be beneficial, including the Turkish Bath.

The House will be heated by means of a Heating Apparatus, so as to make it available as a Winter residence for the most delicate, and will be furnished with everything calculated to minister to the comfort and recreation of the Patients and Visitors.

From estimates which have been made, it is calculated that a House capable of accommodating one hundred and thirty Patients, including Baths, Furniture, and every other thing necessary, may be erected for £21,000; and it is proposed to make the Capital that amount, divided into eight hundred and forty Shares of £25 each.

It is not intended to raise the ordinary charge to Patients above that which has hitherto been paid at Loch-Head (£2 2s. per week), so as to bring the benefits of the Establishment within the reach of the largest possible number; and with this moderate charge, and the advantage of the connexion of a large body of Shareholders, it is calculated that the following numbers may moderately be reckoned on as Patients and Visitors during the year:— for three months, *eighty* per week; other three months, *sixty* per week; other three months, *forty* per week; other three months, *twenty* per week. This would give an average during the year of *fifty* per week, which at £2 each, would yield an annual revenue of £5,200

And deducting expenses as follows:

Provisions	£1,300
Wages	500
Coals and Gas	250

Taxes and Insurance	.	.	.	250
Feu-Duty	.	.	.	.	75
Repairs .	.	.	.	.	75
Advertising	.	.	.	.	100
Medical Superintendent	.	.	.	350
House Steward and Clerk .	.	.	100
Miscellaneous .	.	.	.	.	100

3,100

there would remain this balance £2,100
which is equal to Ten per Cent on the capital.

Four-fifths of the capital have already been subscribed . . .

Note:—The Estimate of the cost of the Building, &c., is as follows:

House and Baths	.	.	.	.	.	. £11,000
Water and Sewerage	.	.	.	.	.	1,200
Heating .	.	.	.	.	.	.	.	530
Painting .	.	.	.	.	.	.	.	500
Lodge, and laying out and enclosing ground .	.	1,000
Furniture .	.	.	.	.	.	.	.	3,500
Consideration to Dr Meikle for Good-will, and which he agrees to take payment of in paid-up Shares of the Company .	.	.	.	.	1,000
Preliminary Expenses	.	.	.	.	.	500

£19,230
Leaving for contingencies 1,770

£21,000

Some intimate observation can be made from an examination of the list of shareholders in March 1867. Dr Meikle held by far the greatest number of shares—value £2,000—of which half represented the £1,000 he had received for goodwill, finding the site and so on. The next largest holder was one, Alexander Stuart, a builder in Aberdeen who had 20 shares. He, it should be said, signed the note appended to the building estimate given above, and with whom some sharp words were exchanged when it was found that the estimates submitted and his final costs did not tally by a considerable amount. Next came the Paton family in Alloa. David Paton, who was in the tweed manufacturing business with his brother James, in Tillicoultry, held 16 shares and his daughter Agnes, who was later to become the second Mrs Meikle, held the same amount, while brother James held eight and a sister, Miss Catherine Paton, Cowden Park, Alloa, held four. Twelve were in the hands of Charles W. Anderson, a merchant in Leith who lived at Ashton, Dalkeith, and who became the first regular Chairman. His connections with Leith and Edinburgh probably brought a number of business people from those two areas into the list, and a surprising number of Galashiels, Peebles and Walkerburn men held shares. One of them, Mr Andrew Buchan, Peebles, was a director for two years, and it may have been his influence which brought three of the Ballantyne family, the woollen manufacturers in Walkerburn, into the Company. The only other Alloa shareholders were the Misses Margaret and Isabella Duncanson, who each held eight shares. I think it is likely that they were related to the Paton family.

Crieff merchants supported the new venture well, and we find grocers, drapers, shoemakers, ironmongers, alongside booksellers, bankers, solicitors and even the distiller from Hosh, J. McCallum. The laird, too, is on the list—Sir Patrick Keith Murray, Bart., of Ochtertyre. The town station master, William Veitch, held one share. Only two individuals in the city of Perth took the opportunity of subscribing. They were John Pullar, St. Leonard's Bank, founder of the "Pullar's of Perth" firm, who was a director of the Hydro for two years, and William Craig, the town clerk.

One man who obviously had faith in Dr Meikle was John Cook, who, with his wife Ann, followed the Doctor from Loch-Head Hydro to Crieff, and became respectively the Hydro Steward and housekeeper. He is noted as holding four shares, price £100, which for a working man was a substantial sum in those days.

William Meikle, a cousin of Dr Thomas, who for ten years was Chairman of the Company, held only eight shares at this time, and his half-brother, Christopher, who ran the Edinburgh Savings Bank as William did the Glasgow Savings Bank, held four.

"Stuart, John, 4 York Terrace, London   10   £250"
This is the sole entry from south of the Border.

At a meeting in May 1867, various management committees were appointed, shares were allotted and the first call of £5, less the £2 deposited, made. Plans for the buildings appeared and Dr Meikle gave explanations. All were approved, except that for the tower, on which judgement was reserved and a separate estimate requested.

At the end of September, 1867, this note appeared:

"Important to Crieff.—We are sure that all who take an interest in the sanitary welfare of Crieff, will be delighted to learn that Dr Meikle, of the Hydropathic Establishment, has in the most handsome manner, offered to the town of Crieff, through the Commissioners, all the waste water from the establishment, for the use of the drains. We trust that not only will this offer be readily and heartily accepted, but that this most timeous supply will help to remove a difficulty that was in the way as to the proper draining of Crieff, and that new steps will be taken to remedy this crying grievance . . ."

This offer was accepted, not with any sense of gratitude, but rather as an obligement to the Hydropathic, and this tone of sourness grew with the passing years to positive bitterness, so that the Commissioners and then the Town Council seemed to find satisfaction in oppressing and thwarting the Hydro Company whenever they could. In this matter of water supply and assessment especially they caused trouble for the directors time and again, over the first 20 years and more.

At times any shareholders who were pessimists must have nursed gloomy forebodings in their breasts, as the Company seemed to be continually meeting trouble, some of it leading to law suits. The years '72 and '73 brought them more than their fair share of those actions, for they were involved in three—two with Crieff Police Commissioners (later the Town Council) and one with the Trustees of the Drummond Estate.

A lease for 19 years of the 54-acre field to the west of the Company's ground had been secured from the Drummond Trustees, and it was hoped to make proper walks through it and to cultivate it and pasture cows in it, one great difficulty being to get milk either in sufficient quantity or of good quality. To help cultivation, waste water from the Hydro was to be used to irrigate the field, but before this could be done an interdict was served on the Manager against laying pipes there or conveying sewage into the field. This last suggestion had never been thought of. The Estate Trustees held the wrong end of the stick, for Lord Ormidale, after lengthy proof, decided in favour of the Company, a judgement which the Judges of the First Division of the Court of Session upheld, with expenses against the pursuers.

The Town Commissioners, who apparently enjoyed seeing the discomfiture of the Hydropathic Company, were steadily taking water assessments from them and not giving any water for these. As if to add insult to injury, after the Company secured the lease of the Knock field, as mentioned above, the Commissioners issued notices inviting the townspeople to meet them in the Knock Park on the occasion of the opening of Crieff Water Works on 29th May 1872. The Manager wrote pointing out the Company's rights in this matter but this was ignored and the Company took it to the Sheriff Court, where the action was dismissed because it was not laid properly against a corporate body. The Sheriff gave the Commissioners expenses. On appeal the Sheriff Principal recalled the interlocutor, dismissed the action as the procession had already taken place, and gave neither party expenses.

The third action was, of course, the appeal against the water assessments and lack of supply, and this, too, the Company lost.

Securing an adequate supply of water caused a great deal of negotiation. Permission had to be obtained from Sir Patrick Keith Murray of Ochtertyre, and also from the Trustees of Lady Willoughby d'Eresby (*née* Drummond), owners of Drummond Castle. There was no difficulty with Sir Patrick, but it took a long time to reach agreement with the Drummond Estates. At a meeting on 8th February 1868, the Chairman had to explain that, in consequence of the excessive delay and difficulty about the wayleave for the water pipe through the Drummond Estate, it had not been possible to hold the general meeting in November as intended. It was left to the two leaders to try to obtain modification and complete agreement.

At last, on 21st April, Mr Anderson (chairman) reported completion of the wayleave for the pipes through the Drummond Estate at the Knock of Crieff, and also of the lease or feu of the ground required for the tank.

In the report of the Directors to the first general meeting of the Company on that same date in 1868, the whole story of the venture is told in brief, including a reference to the water supply.

A field on the Knock of Crieff called Galvelbeg consisting of about sixteen acres was feued from Sir Patrick Keith Murray, Baronet, of Ochtertyre, for the purposes of the Establishment.

After a satisfactory analysis of the *Water*, by Professor Brazier of Aberdeen University, the Conalter Springs were obtained on a lease from Sir Patrick K. Murray. Plans for collecting the Water and conveying it to Galvelbeg were prepared by Mr Robert Anderson, Civil Engineer, who had charge of the introduction of the Supply of Water now in use in Aberdeen.

Way Leave. The right to lay the pipes and to have access at all times to maintain them formed part of the conditions of the Lease so far as the line lay through the grounds of Sir Patrick K. Murray. After leaving the Ochtertyre Estate various routes were considered. That which was ultimately resolved upon lay through part of the Drummond Estate, and was designed in such a way as to cause the least possible severance or interference with that Estate. Notwithstanding this, the negociations regarding that comparatively short portion of the line have been of a most protracted nature, but having at last been brought to a conclusion, and the terms adjusted, the Lease or Feu of that portion of the line has been completed, and the work is being proceeded with.

Working plans having been prepared (from the designs agreed on) for the erection of a Building of the most approved construction to provide the extent of accommodation as at first contemplated, with all appliances for Hydropathic purposes, and with suitable warming and ventilating apparatus, the necessary measurements were obtained, Specifications prepared and

Estimates invited which ultimately resulted in the work being contracted for as follows:

1	Mason Work, by Mr Alex. Stuart, Aberdeen	£8,368	9	8
2	Joiner Work, Messrs Kidd and Son, Dundee	4,851		
3	Ironbeams P. and W. McLellan, Glasgow.	272		
4	Slater A. Drysdale and Son, Crieff . .	392		
5	Plasterer Adams, Dundee . . .	1,360		
6	Plumber and Gasfitter C. Anderson, Crieff	868		
7	Painter and Glazier J. Bruce and Son, Perth	633		
8	Marble Mantelpieces Galbraith and Winton	75		
9	Heating etc. H. Purnell, Glasgow . .	717		
10	Bellhanging J. Brydon and Sons, Edinburgh	246	9	0
11	Excavations A. Laidlaw	180		

Cost of the Bulding £17,962 18 8

The total amount of expenditure shown in the balance sheet at 31st March 1868, was £24,636 10s. 5d.

By the date of this meeting, April 1868, matters were really becoming organised. The House was beginning to shape up nicely. The frontage had a dignified look without severity, the gables at each end and the promise of little turrets at the corners giving an air of Scots baronial architecture, while on the south side there were to be lawns and gardens and on the north a wide courtyard with an entrance to the House having no steps so that invalid carriages could be wheeled straight into the hall from arriving coaches.

It is not easy to pinpoint the exact position of the entrance at this time, but it may have been somewhere near the present drive at the top of Ferntower Road, opposite the little gate leading to the golf course. The main drive by Ewanfield did not exist as the Hydro did not own the ground there, at that time. Dr Meikle was also authorised to spend £100 to bring the grounds into order and to plant with ornamental trees and shrubs.

This most commendable move to improve the amenities around the Hydro followed the presentation in February 1868, by Sir Patrick Keith Murray, of 1800 young trees for planting in the grounds, and he had even sent one of his foresters to assist in that work. This has carned the gratitude of visitors to this day; the beauty of the grounds is not the least of the Hydro's assets.

That first general meeting and the preliminary meeting of the Board had long agenda. Terms to be charged in the Hydro were fixed. Preparations were in hand for about 60 visitors to be housed in the first part of the House to be finished, and it was also decided "to proceed with the whole building so far as to have it all roofed in as soon as possible and, it was hoped, would probably be finished ready for opening entire in March or April 1869."

The speed with which operations were pushed on can be imagined, for on 7th August of that same year (1868) 40 bedrooms were ready *and occupied.* Who the occupants were is not recorded, but it seems likely that most of the Directors and a number of the shareholders would be in the company that enjoyed those first few days of this new venture.

Four days after the opening a meeting was held in the Hydro. The decision to complete the building having been taken at the previous meeting it was now agreed to increase the share capital by £4,000, making it £25,000, and the borrowing powers by another £5,000.

A Mr Smieton, Carnoustie, in 1867 had suggested inaugurating a scheme to help Free Church ministers who wished to holiday or recuperate at the Hydro. He offered to lend £2,000 for this purpose, but though the Company were willing to do this, they could not agree with him the terms of the bond.

Mr David Paton, Alloa and Tillicoultry, now offered to lend the Company £4,000 for the benefit of United Presbyterian ministers and missionaries, and this was accepted on a tentative trial of one year.

Among the other entries under "Income" in the minutes of the meeting is

Contribution by Sir P. K. Murray   £900

August 1868, then, saw the opening of the House to the public, and the local *Herald* announced the great event, although there was no opening ceremony.

Opening of the Hydropathic Establishment.—This fine establishment, as far as it is finished, was open for receiving patients yesterday, and we are glad to hear that a very considerable number took up their abode the first day. The building, both as regards comfort and situation, is such that nothing can surpass it, and no one who has visited the spot and looked from it down the valley below, but must have been entranced with the gorgeous view that it commands. Indeed, we question if there is any other establishment in the kingdom that is so finely planned, with so commanding a situation, and with so lovely scenery around it. The very view from its windows is enough to go far to recover any afflicted patient.

On 5th September 1868, the Chairman congratulated the partners on the success which had attended the Establishment since its opening on 7th August. From a statement of receipt and expenditure for the first 26 days, and an estimate of the annual charges, it appeared that there was already more being earned than should suffice to pay interest on all the capital expected to be required. To encourage the occupation of the House during the winter months the Directors had resolved to allow to partners or their families residing there between 1st October and 1st June next, a discount of 10 per cent, off the regular charges, provided each of the shareholders taking advantage of this offer held not less than £100 of the capital stock, fully paid up, for each individual taking the benefit of this arrangement.

Progress of the work on buildings and roads was inspected at the March meeting in 1869, and Dr Meikle was told to re-engage the staff at whatever pay he judged necessary, to take on extra staff if necessary, and to engage a clerk.

On the vexed question of gratuities the Directors took a novel line. They authorised Dr Meikle "to prohibit by special notice or otherwise the receipt of gratuities by any of the servants of the Company. Agreed that in lieu of such gratuities the servants should receive from the Company allowances in proportion to the success of the concern and the estimate formed of their attention to their respective duties, the desire of the Board being that the interests of every member of the Establishment should be fully cared for. The Finance Committee and the Manager to determine the amount of such allowances."

The revenue as at 17th February showed that there might be a surplus at the end of the financial year on 31st March 1869, so the Board remitted to the Finance Committee to recommend a dividend, if they should see fit to do so.

Prior to the second ordinary general meeting of the Company, held in Glasgow on 6th May 1869, the Directors decided that the registered office of the Company should be changed from 154 St. Vincent Street, Glasgow, to Strathearn House, Crieff. The report of the Board to this meeting revealed that £27,089 13s. 6d. had been received and £21,234 5s. expended on the buildings, ground, water supply, house furnishings, legal charges and good-will. The unexhausted capital was £14,848 14s. 8d., while the balance of obligations upon capital to complete the Establishment, it was believed, would not exceed £8,765 15s.

The revenue account showed a balance in favour of the Company of £770 15s. 8d., with some minor charges to be deducted, and a dividend of 15s. per share was declared. Dr Meikle, Mr and Mrs Cook and the other servants were congratulated, their efforts having been highly appreciated by the visitors.

The final paragraph of the report is rather quaint:

The Directors congratulate the Partners on the prospect of success which is before the Company, and to promote this they would recommend, that when the Establishment is fully opened, the Partners should use all proper means to induce their friends to visit it, as they will thus promote a mutual benefit.

At this meeting Mr Hew Miller, factor on Ochtertyre Estate, and Dr Meikle's friend, was appointed a director, and Provost Brown retired from the Board.

When the extra shares, to bring the capital up to £25,000, were put on the market there were 216 applications and only 158 to be disposed of.

In October 1869 the Chairman, the Manager and Mr Hew Miller were authorised to arrange for "Better 'bus accommodation; also for the erection of Piggery, Byre and a limited extent of stable accommodation when other arrangements might render such erections expedient; also for the erection of a Bowling Alley, or covered space for the patients' outdoor recreation in Winter and bad weather."

Almost a year later the Board were still debating the matter of conveyance from and to the railway station, for many complaints had been received, and it was put to the annual general meeting,

That conveyances and Horses should be purchased, as it appears that the Company would be fully compensated for the outlay.

The same committee was to prosecute "negociations for acquiring additional ground in front of the Establishment, a right of road by the back of Morrison's Academy, and a lease of the field to the west of the Company's property."

Mr Anthony Murray, of Dollerie, one of the local lairds, offered to lease to the Company seven acres of ground to the south of the Hydro grounds, but he seemed to regret the offer for he refused the only terms on which the Directors could take over the ground, and after discussing the matter for two years the Company gave up the struggle. At last, as seen in the report of the Board to the annual general meeting on 4th May 1876, the battle was won.

After more than six years negociation a portion of the land to the south of the Company's ground was feued from Mr Anthony Murray as from Martinmas, 1875; instead of the usual obligation to build, which would have frustrated the purpose for which it was desirable to possess the ground, the sum of £702 4s. 8d. was paid at Martinmas, and the feu is held subject to payment of £40 annually; while the amenity will be greatly improved, a considerable portion of the ground thus obtained will be utilised for garden and other purposes.

The acquisition of more land was an incessant problem. It is amusing to read in the old minutes of attempts to get hold of what came to be known as "the triangle". By the time the Company landed it, it might almost have been "the eternal triangle".

Consideration was given at a meeting on 30th October 1874, whether it would be advisable to make any offer for the Ferntower Grounds. The minute goes on:

Dr Meikle was instructed to offer £30 per annum for a lease of an angular piece of the Plantation (to be fenced in by the Co.) to the north of the grounds of the Establishment, and therewith the right of walking over the Knock—and also along the old road to Perth from the west gate of Ferntower, eastwards, but under obligation to avoid interfering with the House or its amenity.

The Directors were still worrying that bone at the beginning of this century and ultimately got possession at Martinmas 1902, 28 years after the first approach.

Here, also, appears the earliest hint of the desirability of access to the Knock.

A deputation from the Board went to see the directors of the Caledonian Railway Co., to discuss cuts that had been imposed in the services to Crieff, and they were successful in getting the Railway Company to run a midday train which answered the purpose the deputation had in mind. Request —discussion—request granted. Those *were* the days.

Mention has been made of the troubles that arose over the water supply and water assessment, and in 1875 the Manager received instructions to adhere to the offer already made for assessment. To cut a long and tedious story short, I may say that, despite the fact that the Company paid what they considered legally necessary, the Town Commissioners took them to Court in 1876, and in 1878 Sheriff Barclay gave decree and expenses against the Company. Although they appealed against this they lost the case and were advised to drop the matter, which they did. Thus ended the first fight with the town in the matter of water. More skirmishing was to come.

A steadier pressure of water for working the hoists and engines was required in 1881, so it was decided to lay a five-inch iron pipe from the tank on the Knock to the north side of the House. In the following year, in an endeavour to reach an understanding with the Town Council, the Board were so frustrated that they authorised the Chairman and the Manager "to take such steps as may be necessary to get such a clause inserted in the Public Health Amendment Act, now before Parliament, as may give the Company some measure of Justice". Dr Meikle wrote to the Member of Parliament about this but the reply indicated no hope of relief.

In October 1883, it was agreed to apply again to the town for a supply of water, especially during repairs to the Company's works. The bickering went on; letters flew between the two sides. By 1885 the Directors were willing to submit the questions of the connection with Crieff water supply to Mr Ritchie, C.E. (Civil Engineer) and to leave it to the Chairman and Manager to settle the terms with the local authority for the use of the pipe from the tank on the Knock. The town would have none of this.

Apparently the threat of yet another Court action appeared, for the *Strathearn Herald* gave this account of a meeting of the Town Water Board, early in 1888:

THE HYDROPATHIC COMPANY AND THEIR WATER SUPPLY— THREATENED ACTION

At last meeting a letter was read from the Hydropathic Company in regard to the water supply to their Establishment, and offering the following terms:—(1) to pay £15 per annum; (2) to pay in addition thereto for all the water the Company take as per meter and at agreed rates, and by a pipe one to two inches bore. The Board agreed to grant a one-inch pipe to the Company for a supply for domestic purposes, and from the top of the main. The Clerk now stated that he had written to the Company, in terms of the instructions given him at last meeting, and the following was the answer he had received:

194 West George St.,
Glasgow, 28th Feb. 1888

Strathearn Hydropathic

Dear Sir,—I received yours of the 15th curt. in answer to mine of 17th Oct., and which I submitted to the Directors. Permit me to say that a reply might and ought to have been sent after the first meeting of the Committee, instead of allowing four months to elapse. . . .

The Directors maintain that the Company is entitled to a due and adequate supply of water for the purposes of the Establishment, and they will insist on their rights. Your Board gives a ¾-inch bore to houses rented at £50, even in the low level, while

they will only give a 1-inch bore to the Company who are rented
at £1250. . . . Should it be found that the supply be insufficient,
the Company will take proceedings to obtain the supply of water
to which they are legally entitled.

Let me add—My Company have hitherto paid water rates to
the amount of between £400 and £500 without receiving any
water; and considering that the Company is rated many times
larger than any of the inhabitants, it appears to the Directors a
mockery to style (as one of the Commissioners is reported to have
done) the proposal of your Board as "equitable justice".
(Laughter) Dr Meikle will arrange with the Committee as to the
introduction of the water.   I am,

Yours truly,
James Alexander.

James Alexander, a Glasgow lawyer, and a director of
the Company had been asked to handle this matter.

From this period onwards the stormy waters seem to have
subsided and only when the hydro-electric scheme came to be
built did the problems over the water supply again come to
the fore.   But, that, as Kipling used to say, is another story.

The Establishment, as may be realised, required a lot of
water, and even in the very early days, when numbers of
visitors were not great, some alarm was felt that there might
be a shortage of water even after the reservoir had been
enlarged.   On this account Captain Colquhoun of Clathick
was asked for the use of one of the feeders to the Clathick
Burn, and this he at once handsomely granted, refusing to
accept any remuneration for it.   "The Directors expressed
their deep gratitude."

PROBLEMS AND PROGRESS

"So he with difficulty and labour hard
Moved on . . . ."

MILTON

The completed house had been opened to visitors in July 1869, and before that date and for weeks after, applications for admission poured in so that a far bigger building could have been filled. Naturally, the energies of the whole staff were taxed, but "the satisfaction given to those who came seems to have been universal".

The Turkish bath was opened that September, and may have induced some people to remain throughout the winter.

The comfortable temperature maintained in the corridors and throughout the House during the winter months has been noticed by several who availed themselves of treatment during that season. The advantages to be derived from Hydropathy, at that period of the year, where such special provision is made for the comfort of Invalids, ought to be more generally known.

The Hydro never brought the name of Crieff into prominence as a centre of pure hydropathy, in the way that Drs Wilson and Gully did for Malvern, but there is not the slightest doubt that thousands of individuals who came to Strathearn House on account of their health went away feeling much the better for their stay there. And this was not only by reason of the baths, douches and treatment received, but also the quiet and peaceful atmosphere in and around the House at all times. One lady has written to me:

"Dr Thomas Henry Meikle was a unique person and it was that, more than anything else, that made the Hydro a unique place. He believed that, to have a healthy mind and body one must have a healthy soul and to this end he provided spiritual sustenance along with medical and therapeutic treatment. As you probably know, there were Morning and Evening Prayers and Services on Sundays. I don't see how anyone could look at the grandeur and serenity of the mountains from the Hydro and not believe in God."

That sentiment, had it been openly expressed to them, would have re-echoed from the minds of a huge percentage of the visitors, especially in the first fifty years of the Hydro's existence and there are many even today who still uphold that idea. Morning and evening prayers are not now held, but in the months when the beneficiaries of the Meikle, Paton and Smieton funds are living in the House, morning prayers are held after breakfast and there is always a service of worship on Sunday evenings, usually very well attended.

As early as 1870 the Board were beginning to note the possibility of keeping cows for supplies of milk. The advantage which had already accrued from the keeping of pigs gave them further ideas and they authorised the erection of suitable buildings for these purposes.

A dividend of 35s. per share was approved that year and the congratulations of the Directors to the shareholders were passed once more.

This success [they said], may be expected to continue, not from the many fitful visits received during the short time after opening, before the Winter came upon us, and which have been experienced during last month [April, 1870] but by those who need rest from the over-exertion which the customs of society entail on so many, taking the use of the Establishment for a certain period of time.

The conveyance of passengers to and from the railway station in Crieff still caused much inconvenience, so Dr Meikle asked the Post Office if it would be possible to connect the Hydro with the station by wire. He was told that this could be done and the Government would supply all necessary apparatus for £18 per annum, under contract for three years. Immediate connection was asked for to save running the omnibus unnecessarily, and it was also decided that, in winter when things were quiet, the horses would be used to bring coals up from the town in two spring carts, to be purchased for this and other uses.

One surprising side issue to the picking up of visitors at the station lies in the arrangement with the Railway Company that, for one shilling a year—so I am told—the stationmaster at Crieff would let the Hydro office know, by means of the private wire between the two points, whether there would be visitors for the Hydro off the next train. Apparently, before reaching Crieff [later Gleneagles] Junction, the guard went along the train asking if there were any passengers for Crieff Hydro. He then informed the stationmaster at the Junction who wired the stationmaster at Crieff who, in turn, told the Hydro. Appropriate transport was then sent down—a coach for passengers and a box cart for luggage. J. J. Bell in his reminiscences, comments on this arrangement. There is, it goes without saying, the story that the horse pulling the cart refused to pass the Crown Hotel bar without stopping.

Most visitors arrived at the House by rail though, in the early years of this century, the odd person or party would come by car. And that *was* a sensation. Dr Meikle himself owned one of the first cars in Crieff.

Much earlier an unfortunate accident [which was purely accidental caused by the awkwardness of the turn at Water Lane] having occurred, Mr Miller and the Manager were requested to arrange as to the Damage.

This is all that the minutes say about this incident, but the *Strathearn Herald* of Oct. 22nd. 1880, has more.

Carriage Accident.—On Tuesday morning an accident occurred at the foot of the Water Wynd, whereby two men narrowly escaped with their lives. It seems that the omnibus which runs from the Hydropathic Establishment to the railway station came into violent collision with an Irish car which was being driven by a young man. The car was smashed to pieces and rendered useless, and the pole of the omnibus broken. The men and horses, however, escaped with very little injury.

The *Herald* at this time was frequently printing snippets of news about the Hydro, and in one of these, after speaking of the new telegraph wire between Hydro and station, the editor hears, also, that the Directors are proposing to erect a gymnasium "at a very considerable cost." In fact, they were going to add a recreation room, billiard room and bowling alley as well, the cost of them all not to exceed £1000, and work to be started immediately.

The laird (Sir Patrick Murray) still found opportunities to assist the Establishment: in the previous summer he had presented a boat on Ochtertyre Loch—the loch just a mile or so out of the town on the Comrie road and lying below Ochtertyre House. He had thrown his policies open to visitors to the Hydro at all seasons and given them this rowing boat, so the Directors ordered Stothart and McGregor to build a boathouse for it. Ochtertyre also gave permission for pipes to be laid to intercept water from a higher level than the reservoir which had contained only 1 ft. 11 ins. of water on 1st September 1870.

Sir Patrick married in the autumn of this year and the Board sent his wife a drawing-room timepiece and vases as a wedding present.

As may have been noticed from the foregoing, the year 1870 really kept Dr Meikle and his staff hustling and one other important matter he and the Chairman and Mr Hew Miller had to tackle was an approach to the Drummond Estate for a more convenient access to the Hydro. When the new approach road did come it came through the ground leased from Mr Anthony Murray of Dollerie—the few acres immediately in front of the House—and led into the road known as Ewanfield; in effect, the present main approach to the Hydro. But the years had flown since the first request to the Drummond Estate, for the avenue above Ewanfield was only decided on in April 1877, and completed the following year.

In 1870, several other decisions taken are worthy of note. Dr Meikle got a £70 rise of salary—he started at £350 plus various perquisities—and Mr and Mrs John Cook, steward and housekeeper, who appear to have been on a joint salary, went up from £120 to £180—very good money for those days.

The valuation put on the Hydro by the assessor was £300, but this was to be appealed against.

A licence to sell stamps was to be sought, a move which ultimately brought about the installation of a Post Office in the House itself, with its own postmark. An article in *The Stamp Magazine* a number of years ago states:

One of the most select hotels in Scotland is the Strathearn Hydro in Crieff, Perthshire, and in Edwardian times it, too, had its own post office. Date stamps inscribed either "The Hydropathic, Crieff" or "Crieff Hydropathic" were used on parcels and telegrams, though I have not seen either of them used on letters or postcards. .

I am inclined to think that the Post Office was placed in the Hydro long before Edward VII came to the throne, for it was not a new idea to have such an office in a hotel or inn, even in 1870.

After the business had been operating for two years, with all the vital decisions to be taken and a great deal of work to be done, it was decided that the Directors should set aside £120 for their own services. As there were ten of them this was not over-payment at £12 a man for two years. At the same time their number came down to nine, and in April 1871, they recommended to the annual general meeting that the number should be seven and their remuneration fixed at £50. The Board then were:

Mr Charles W. Anderson, *Chairman*

Mr. David Paton	Mr William Meikle
Mr Francis Fulton, Leith	Mr John MacLeish, Crieff
Mr Hew Miller	Mr George Rough

Twelve pounds per man was not a great deal, and perhaps they realised this themselves, for "in consideration of the interest taken by the Directors in the Business of the Company, they shall have the privilege of residing in the Establishment for a fortnight during each year free of charge. For the like reason and the special services rendered by the present Chairman of the Co., he and one of his family shall have the benefit of the Establishment for whatever time they see fit; the like privilege and the like reasons being hereby accorded to Mr Wm. Meikle".

Many of the people of Crieff knew that there was a right-of-way running from the town over the west shoulder of the

Knock to Monzie, and it appears that it was used on Sundays by some of the townsfolk walking over to the kirk at Monzie. The last part of their walk took them through Monzie Estate, and, whether because hooligans were causing damage or whether on account of human perversity—thrawnness, we would say in Scotland—the laird had fences put up across the right of way. Naturally, this roused the wrath of Crieff and a crowd walked over and tore the obstructions down, a proceeding which happened more than once. In the interests of their visitors, the Hydro directors wished all rights of way protected and kept open. It is not easy to walk to Monzie Kirk by this route to-day.

About 25 years later the Board had to protect their own amenities. They gave instructions that the grounds were to be kept clear of youths from Crieff, especially on Sundays. That, and an objection they voiced strongly in 1886 about the grounds being used as a short-cut by workmen—their own and others—and as a playground by children of employees, were the only times noted in the old minutes that the Board had jealously to guard their lands and the amenities on behalf of their guests.

As the years went on and numbers of visitors grew, one of the Articles of Association dealing with the provision of a separate residence for the Manager rose to the surface.

So Strathearn Leigh was built and to-day part of it makes a quiet annex for a dozen or more visitors. The funds for this building came from the second loan (£2000) by Mr Paton for the benefit of U.P. Church ministers.

At this same time (1877) a partition had been prepared to divide the dining room so that the southern end might be used as a drawing room during the winter months. The screen had a permanent appearance but could be easily removed if more seats were required in the dining room. These and other alterations in the House including the heating of the upper corridors, were very much approved by visitors and, according to the minutes, the new road by Ewanfield gave a much better view of the House and country around; a remark which shows that there can have been no trees or houses to obscure the view.

In the matter of views the Company were lucky to have Sir Patrick Keith Murray as a neighbour, for he gave them permission, once they had got possession of the field to the west of the building, to extend the path through that field onwards through Culcrieff, "opening up to the visitors, the grand view to the west, as well as the freedom of the field so far as not under crop". That was in 1874, and five years later he practically gave them a large greenhouse. Dr Meikle had decided that he could not pay more than £20 as it was going to cost so much to remove and re-erect, so he had let the matter drop. Sir Patrick, however, gave it to the Company for £20.

The Hydro has relied on satisfied guests to advertise its advantages and therefore has rarely advertised itself publicly. The first mention of such an idea occurs in 1881 when Dr Meikle took it upon himself to decline to pay for advertising copy in either the N.B. Railway or the Caledonian Railway Companies' Tourist Guides.

One of the amenities referred to from time to time was the stabling of visitors' horses and coaches, and more space for this purpose had to be found. Buildings erected for stabling were not going to be wasted, however, as some of them came later to be adapted for housing motor cars. When you think of the motor car in 1902 does it not make you marvel at the "with-it-ness" of the Directors of that date? Yet another regular charge on the Company was the erection of cottages for employees, so that in their report to the annual general meeting of 7th May 1883, the Board said that four more cottages were being built, and attached to them are four rooms intended to be used by coachmen or grooms who might come with visitors.

Numbers of people coming to stay at the Hydro had tended to remain low after the City of Glasgow Bank failure in 1878, and the Directors, though always optimistic, had to admit that business was not as good as it should be. It fluctuated, of course, and dividends never dropped below seven per cent. and every two or three years a small bonus came along to keep shareholders happy.

Expenses went on all the time, and building concrete

walls along the boundary of the Company's property accounted for quite a sum.

One property which had annoyed the Directors more than somewhat was that corner on Ferntower Road where Victoria Terrace and Knock Road join it. Commonly called "Paul Campbell's Corner", it housed a very small selection of livestock, and, from what I have heard and read, was nothing less than a very dirty and probably smelly farmyard, sunk about a couple of feet below the level of the roadway. Visitors to the Hydro passed that corner on their way to the Hydro and it surely cannot have made a good impression on anyone Who Paul Campbell was I do not know, but it looks as though he was a farmer in a very small way; perhaps only a dairyman. No matter. The Crieff Mineral Well Company—they brought the mineral water from a little well at Cowgask, Madderty, I was told by Mrs Macphail, Kiplonie, Crieff, in 1966, when she was 93— at last bought the corner, and in recognition of the improvement effected by them and in order to encourage them, the Directors took four £5 shares in that company in the name of the Manager.

CASTLE IN THE AIR

Build on, and make thy castles high and fair.
LONGFELLOW

Dr Meikle's dreams were coming true. The Hydropathic grew busier and busier. Where could he find space for more bedrooms? More dining room space? More everything?

In the second prospectus, they estimated the numbers in a year as around the 2600 mark. That was a very close guess, but of course, all sorts of other considerations came into the reckoning—an uneven spread-over with the summer months crowded and the winter months quiet; higher terms than those that had been proposed and kept for a few years; and so on.

Now the demand was for more and more accommodation.

In 1872 the total number of visitors for the year (April 1, 1872 to March 31, 1873) was 2545, but in the next twelve months, despite the increased charges, the figure shot up to 3267. The total was mounting each year.

No totals are given for the previous years but in May 1871, the minutes remark that during several months of 1870 visitors greatly exceeded the number expected, and

". . . . . while the Directors trust that no such sad cause, as that which led many tourists to visit Scotland last Autumn instead of going to the Continent, will occur again, they hope that as the current year has opened well, not withstanding the inclemency of the weather during much of last month, it may be as successful as the last."

The "sad cause" was the Franco-Prussian war which, with the siege of Paris, must certainly have been a deterrent to visiting that gay city.

As someone remarked to me, the Hydro assimilates change, and from its first year improvements, additions and alterations kept staff and workmen employed. By 1872 more accommodation was being looked for and it was decided to convert the large space over the wings into attic bedrooms.

An "Ice House" also became a necessity, and this had been foreseen by Dr Meikle, for in the wall of the north side of the building provision had been made for access to such an apartment, which was to be built underground. A concrete meat safe, as suggested by the Manager, had to be fashioned, and as the manual hoist for raising and lowering dishes between kitchen and serving pantry constituted a risk, the Directors authorised the installation of an hydraulic one.

A review of the wages of the men employed by the Company took place and Dr Meikle gave increases as he thought right. Similar reviews took place at regular intervals. He himself was empowered to charge 10s. 6d. as a fee for consultations, as this privilege was being abused. Ministers, teachers and other such exceptional cases were exempt.

It could never be said that the Chairman and his Directors did not appreciate Dr Meikle's contribution towards the success of the venture. Their report to the Company meeting in May 1874, also made that plain to the shareholders.

Although the Directors never doubted that, with sufficient capital and good management, the concern would be ultimately successful, yet they felt from the first that much risk attended bringing it into working order; the fact that there were almost no extras incurred in completing the building is due principally to the forethought of Dr Meikle and the laborious pre-arrangement and adaptation by him of every part for the purposes intended, so that no material alteration was required during the progress of the work, and the early opening, by which it became so soon remunerative, was thus accomplished, the place being unique, no professional architect could have produced such a design without probably much greater expense being incurred, and all Dr Meikle's able services in this primary department, the erection of the premises, have never yet been duly considered.

This eulogy arose from an unexpected move on Thomas Meikle's part. He had suggested, eight months previously, that he should lease the whole premises and property of the Company for a period of seven years. A bombshell of this kind had to receive careful treatment, and it was given that. The greatly increased anxiety and responsibility that would devolve on Dr Meikle was pointed out; also the fundamental changes that would be needed in the constitution of the Company. There seemed to the Directors to be many serious obstacles against such a move, and instead they proposed to increase the Doctor's salary to £500, in addition to board and residence as before; and further, that whatever clear profit appeared at the end of the business year, after sufficient had been put aside for improvements, depreciation and renewal, should be applied, first in providing a dividend up to seven per cent., second, that any profit exceeding that amount should be equally divided in three parts, the first as a bonus to members, the second payable to Dr Meikle "in consideration of his success in so promoting the prosperity of the Company", and the third should be added to reserve or form a dividend guarantee fund.

All this was agreed at the meeting, and the immediate result was that shareholders received a dividend of £1 15s. plus a bonus of 5s. 6d. per share, equal to eight and one-tenth per cent., and Dr Meikle got £278 17s., while £283 13s. 11d. went to start the dividend guarantee scheme.

Bookings during the first years of the Establishment had been so numerous that the office staff had had to obtain temporary accommodation outside the House for some visitors. This was not a convenient arrangement, so, in 1872 a cottage was rented, an expense which was repaid by the use made of it. The additional attic bedrooms were expected to do away with the need to rent outside rooms.

The need for booking rooms in the town for Hydro visitors is not mentioned again until the period of the Second World War, when the Hydropathic was requisitioned, and, under the various Trusts for the clergy, arrangements were made to house beneficiaries in private dwellings in Crieff.

Extensive improvements to the baths in 1873 made them, the Board thought, equal if not superior to any elsewhere. It was believed, too, that if the comfort throughout the House during the winter months were more generally known, many invalids might be more benefited by coming to the Hydro than by going to southern climes.

The rush of bookings meant that Dr Meikle was constantly looking for areas of the building where he could erect more bedrooms, and towards the end of '73 he made plans to add a gentlemen's room, an addition to the east wing of ten bedrooms and a billiard room. The smokers had again raised the question of a smoking room, and ultimately gained their point.

There are frequent remarks about extensions being found very beneficial, and two years later the Directors were considering plans for extending the drawing-room and dining-room, and raising the drawing-room ceiling about five feet. Wm. Donaldson and Sons, builders, Crieff, estimated £998 for each of these rooms, "subject to a deduction of £30 from each sum . . . if allowed to take down and utilise the whole of the South gables."

The meeting having maturely considered the subject, including the fact of insufficient accommodation for the visitors to the House for nearly six months last year, and fully more than that period this year, also the unwholesome condition of the rooms, especially the Drawing-room during the hot season as well as at other times when there was a great influx of visitors—and that every effort should be used in the interest of the Company, notwithstanding the great expense, to promote the comfort of the visitors during the season when most if not all the profit is made. . . . resolved that the proposed alterations and extensions were imperatively required . . .

So rapidly did the builder get down to it that within six months the drawing-room and rooms above it were ready and the dining room wing was far advanced.

Further references to the bad conditions in drawing- and dining-rooms appear in the report to the annual meeting in May, 1876, as follows:

The influx of visitors during the summer months, when the highest rate is charged, was in excess even of the previous year, so that in both these years especially the unwholesome closeness of the Drawing Room was felt by all, and complained about by many; and at the season the accommodation in the Dining room was so insufficient that the servants could not wait properly, and the visitors were inconveniently crowded at table, while about 30 of them had to dine in the Recreation room.

Yet another improvement in the House was the installation of a new heating apparatus, extending the central heating to the upper corridors; thus the excessively cold winter of '78 was comfortably withstood, to the delight of those visitors residing throughout the winter months.

1878 had been a poor year and the dividend dropped from £1 15s. and a bonus of 5s. 6d. per share in 1877 to £1 10s. per share (6 per cent.). The number of visitors dropped from the highest ever—3907—to 2903, for three reasons, the Directors thought. The first was the opening of several new hydropathics; the second, the failure of the City of Glasgow Bank; and thirdly, the extraordinarily severe and protracted winter. The Board appealed to everyone to practise every possible economy. Better conditions prevailed in the next year and numbers went up to 2993, but owing to shorter average periods of residence the income went down a little.

Ten years later (1888) a series of proposals for additional rooms was approved. A large day nursery for the children, which would also be suitable for servants of visitors having meals; a room or small hall for prayer meetings or Bible readings; and eight good bedrooms were all to be built at the east end of the House. A second turret was erected, on the north-east corner of the building. In the following year, the Directors' report stated that a new bakery, dairy and store rooms in the basement, spacious hall and children's room on the ground floor, and on the first and second floors four good sized rooms and three attics would be ready before the busy time began.

Electric lighting was introduced into the public rooms.

The Directors, after going and inspecting the Perthshire Dyeing and Cleaning Works at Dallerie—on the south fringe of the town and near the River Earn—bought them as they stood, with "all the movables belonging to Captain Dundas". The reason for this purchase, made in 1890, was, of course, that the laundry facilities at the Hydro had long been inadequate for the growing needs of the business. The price of £2893 10s. 7d. included three acres of ground, buildings covering over half an acre, a 40-h.p. steam engine and a variety of apparatus for washing, drying, calendering, ironing tables, sewing machines, etc. It was proposed to add a carpet beating machine as the work of beating the large and numerous carpets in the Establishment meant a great tax on the staff.

An unanticipated use of an empty dwelling house at Dallerie came not long after the purchase of the property. The house was used as a sanatorium for a visitor who had fever, "thereby preventing it from spreading, and saving the 'stampede' of the 200 in the Hydro at the time, and serious injury to the whole season".

Two years later, the dining-room having been widened two feet, the vestibule seven feet, the floor of the recreation room relaid in oak, the Directors were asking approval of further extensions—and this time they really were going to town.

. . . further extensions, some of which have been begun: New smoking room; new billiard room. An extension to the Dining room, on pillars, to the front of the House, and the addition of from 30 to 40 bedrooms to the north-west of the House.

Here, then, were the west wing—the New Wing as most people still call it—and that part of the dining-room projected on to the front of the main dining-room. The money to pay for these came by borrowing, the mason's estimate accepted for the new wing alone amounting to £2158 10s. The money borrowed was to be repaid over the next few years.

The new wing was opened in August 1894, and with the increased and superior accommodation afforded by it, during August, September and October, and over the New Year holidays, what would have proved "a deficit" has turned out "a surplus" year . . . The extension of the Dining room has also proved very satisfactory, accommodating 80 additional visitors.

In this way, gradually and systematically, improvements were undertaken, and the "modern" trend always kept in view. Here is one comment on that aspect:

It will be 25 years on 7th August next (1893), since the Establishment was opened, and during that long period it has had a fair share of success, but this age we live in becomes more luxurious, which means that better food, better rooms, better furnishings and better surroundings than were necessary 25 years ago, are now expected if not demanded, without proportionate increase in the charges, and yet the only hope of securing continued success seems to lie in trying to meet these demands so far as possible, and the larger rooms in the new addition, and the other improvements will, it is hoped, enable the Establishment to maintain the prosperity it has hitherto enjoyed, and prove itself a real boon to jaded and suffering humanity.

That might have been written at the Directors' last meeting instead of nearly 75 years ago.

If business improved fairly steadily, at least the Board could not be blamed for keeping up the dividend at the expense of keeping up the House. As well as a long list of repairs and improvements to be done in 1896 it was decided to spend £2000 on the overhauling and renovating of the baths and also to put carpets on most of the stairs and corridors and curtains in the "superior rooms". Those "superior rooms" attracted a great deal of attention and demand, helping materially to augment the income, but they were to be over-shadowed by the next big addition.

Towards the end of 1900 a discussion took place in the boardroom on the erection of a Winter Garden. The idea found approval but erection was delayed at that time. Talk of this scheme went on in the following years and it was not till the beginning of 1903 that the Chairman—Dr Meikle now—proposed that they should utilise the large open space below the planned winter garden for nine additional bedrooms, and under these a swimming pool with dressing boxes and one or two rain baths. This splendid idea was discussed and approved. Work was begun in the spring of 1903 but owing to unfortunate delays was not ready, as had been hoped, for mid-summer. In fact, it was opened at Easter 1904, and greatly admired. Ten more bedrooms, not nine as forecast, were in use for the busiest time of summer, but the swimming pool did not function till Easter of 1905, the year in which it was agreed to enlarge the dining-room again to give the present annex (the "House of Lords"), and to have the pantry extended greatly. The annex came into use early in 1907.

Those were the last really big developments, but the year 1931 brought rather an alarming report. The main south wall of the Hydro was found to be off plumb so that measures had to be taken to strengthen the walls throughout the central section of the building, a job that was done with great skill and a minimum of inconvenience, though one jocular remark suggested that if they removed the struts the Hydro would just roll down the hill into Crieff.

Soon after this there began the lengthy process of providing bathrooms on the different floors of the House and then of putting hot and cold water basins into all bedrooms. Up to this time (and indeed later) "the bath procession", as one delightful person told me, had become one of the social events of the day. She said:

"We put on our prettiest dressing gowns and walked along the corridor to the lift, meeting and greeting friends and acquaintances on the way, many of them heading in the same direction. Down we went in the lift—men and women together—to the basement where our paths divided. The men went to the left and the ladies to the right. I always tried to go down early to have a 'crack' with the bathmaids. They lived in a kind of kitchen place, all tiled, and they sat there waiting for someone to come down, when one of them would go and run a bath for the visitor. They had one or two canaries in cages and of course I tried to get the birds to sing and was delighted if they did.

"There were two rows of baths on each side of the passage-way and the baths were separated only by drapings so that, if a friend joined you, you could have adjacent baths, and although you could not see one another, you could converse through the curtains."

Further recollections of a period shortly before bathmen and maids became redundant tell of two of the bathmaids who were sisters. Strict disciplinarians, like the bathmen, they ruled their domain with unquestioned authority. Thus they could be pretty formidable to those who did not know them. In fact, they had the kindest hearts, and long after their retirement to a house in the grounds they welcomed visits from former patrons and laughed with them over old times. Their brother George was chief bathman and spokesman of a fine phrase (whether original or not) that amused many of the guests—"All haste is vulgar".

It is also told of him that, when the House was full of ministers of the Church, one of them, departing gave him a specially generous tip. George, expressing thanks, said, "That's more than I'll get from the whole General Assembly".

In the bathhouse at one point a rope hung from the roof and this the person receiving treatment reached up to and held with both hands while being sponged or douched under the arms. "It's like the hangman's noose," one man suggested; "There's no hanging here, Sir, I'd rather see you married," replied George.

I hope these reminiscences conjure up all kinds of pleasant memories for those who knew the Hydro at this time.

Upkeep costs of the building were running fairly high, what with reinforcing the south wall, replacing the cupola above the Winter Garden, and putting hot and cold water into 172 bedrooms. The cost of that last item was £4370, which included two calorifiers and tanks.

Arising out of the first installation of bathrooms on the various floors, it appears that these rooms were not, as now, available for everyone. Each was let with a bedroom, the tenant of which had the key, so that it constituted, in effect, a private bathroom.

And here mention may be made of the present position. Private bathrooms have been created by reducing the size of a number of the larger rooms, and wherever possible this progressive plan is still being executed, but to instal bathrooms into even a majority of the bedrooms would mean the loss of much sleeping accommodation and would elevate considerably the Hydro terms of residence. By reason of the large numbers that can be accommodated in the House, terms have always been kept appreciably lower than those of other hotels of comparable quality in Scotland; and at a level which has been recognised by a large section of Scottish and English holidaymakers as very good value. It is seldom, even when the House is full, that one cannot have a bath when desired, and it is a great pleasure to find, at all hours of day or night, boiling hot water gushing from one tap, and from the other, cold cold water ready to temper it.

FROM A NEEDLE TO AN ANCHOR

"The time has come, the Walrus said, to talk of many things,
Of shoes, and ships, and sealing wax, and cabbages and kings."
LEWIS CARROLL

Laundry maids were included among the staff employed for the first 20 years but with the increasing numbers of guests and the demands of those guests this ancillary operation began to get out of hand. We have seen how the Board bought the Perthshire Dyeing and Cleaning Works at Dallerie, so not long after that the Company was in the laundry business. Needless to say, by the time the works had been overhauled, some new machinery installed and the wheels were turning, it became obvious that the plant had the capacity to handle a lot more work than the Hydro would provide. In this way, a service for the townspeople came into being—a service which took on a much broader base in 1966 when the Company bought over the Strathearn Steam Laundry Company and amalgamated the two concerns.

As has been shown, Sir Patrick Keith Murray, Bart., of Ochtertyre, had been a most kindly neighbour, so on the occasion of his eldest son's 21st birthday, the Directors decided to present him with four shares in the Company— nominal value, £100, but actually worth a good deal more as dividends of around nine per cent. were being paid annually at this time.

In the midst of all the joyful celebrations on 8th April 1893, Mr William Meikle, Dr Meikle, Mr Hew Miller, Mr James Alexander and Mr Robert Ewan (architect and now a Director) went to Ochtertyre and presented the young laird with a silver casket which bore on one side a representation in relief of scenery near Ochtertyre, and on the other a picture of the Hydropathic. The casket contained, of course, the certificates for the four shares. Mr Meikle expressed the pleasure of the Directors in being given the chance to show their high respect and esteem towards the House of Ochtertyre. Sir Patrick had thrown open to them the grounds of his house and the gates of Ochtertyre were open summer and winter, day and night—"like the gates of Heaven themselves".

Mr William Keith Murray, in reply, said that Crieff Hydro was the only hydro that really did pay, and that was due more to the skill with which it was managed by Dr Meikle than to all the scenery of Crieff put together.

Indications have been given at several points of Sir Patrick Murray's generosity. One instance of this which posed a pretty problem for the author for some months is minuted in 1884, as follows:

"Mr Hew Miller, Factor for Sir Patrick Keith Murray, Bart. of Ochtertyre, intimated that Sir Patrick is willing to make over 3 ft. 9 inches in No. 81 seat in the Parish Church of St. Michael, in consideration of the lands of Galvelbeg feued by him to this Co."

This gesture of good-will simply indicated that the Laird wished to pass on to a heritor—someone in Scotland who is a landholder—part of the Parish Church pew space to which he, Sir Patrick, had an automatic right. As Dr Meikle had feued Galvelbeg from him in order to build the Hydropathic there, he was offering him two seats in pew No. 81.

Dr Meikle, having been Manager and Medical Superintendent for 25 years, his son, Dr Gordon Meikle, was appointed to assist him generally. Dr Meikle then became a Director in place of Gordon. John Macharg, C.A., 69 Buchanan Street, Glasgow, was appointed auditor, and to-day the auditor is still a Macharg, a nephew of the former.

To secure amenity, part of the Knock was feued from the Drummond Estates. The Manager had bought the villa, Overdale, lying to the west of the grounds, for £1,600. This he did on behalf of the Company in connection with the feuing of the adjoining ground from the Drummond Estates. He had advanced the price on loan to the Company and this meant that now they owed him £4000, two other loans being for £2030 and £370.

The feu on the Knock extended to just over 14 acres.

For the first time the numbers of visitors had gone over the 5000 mark in one year—and that was without the extra bedrooms that the new, west wing, was going to give.

Trouble with the hydraulically operated passenger hoist brought the suggestion that the reservoir should be extended.

1895. The smoke from the furnaces has been conveyed away from the Establishment in an underground channel made in 18 , and a steel chimney 50' high and 2' in diameter erected at the top of the grounds, about 300 feet from the House. (The year is not given.)

This was replaced by a brick chimney in 1903.

There you have the chimney in the woods to the north-east of the tennis courts. The next refinement in the House came with the replacement by silver plated tea and coffee pots of "the present tin ones".

The Directors had very great pleasure at the A.G.M. of 1896 in submitting the most favourable report they had yet been able to give. "Arrivals" nearly reached 6,000 and the revenue went up £2732 over the previous year. "An unusual number of patients made prolonged stays, of 2 to 6 months, which materially assisted in promoting this success."

Another advance of a different kind was the appointment of "a Miss Mitchell as a shorthand typewriter to help in the office".

Mr William Meikle, now aged 81, resigned from the Chair and had Dr Thomas appointed in his place.

A suggestion that the Falls of Barvick be utilised to generate electricity for the Hydro came from someone the following year and became a reality before 1900. Electricity and electric gadgets were becoming commonplace. Another telephone in a silence cabinet was added to the facilities of the House.

A palm hothouse found favour and came into use early in 1906. This is one feature of the Winter Garden that has almost disappeared. For many years, as older "regulars" —indeed, some also not so old—will recall, palm plants which grew to quite a height were profusely dotted about in the Winter Garden giving the pleasant atmosphere of a conservatory to the place. These were grown under glass and then transferred to the House when of a suitable size.

At this same time the dining-room annex appeared, "so that smaller dining tables might be used", states the minute. Revolving doors took the place of swing doors in the vestibule.

A chef de cuisine—the very first—was engaged, and the change seemed to give satisfaction to the visitors, who had been complaining about the food. This was Mr Gillies A. Calazel, who resigned in 1922 after 15 years' service to go to Peebles Hydro, of which he ultimately became proprietor.

In addition to the normal work-a-day problems the Board required to keep abreast of legislation that might affect them as a Company and employer of labour. For example, in May 1907, owing to a new law on liability, they reported that they had had to insure the whole staff against accident. It was just as well, too, for in building the new dam on the Barvick to obtain a higher head of water, two accidents occurred, one of them fatal, but both were covered by insurance. As many legal matters arose in the course of each year, it was decided to pay Mr Swanston Drysdale, lawyer in Crieff, who, previously had been consulted in an advisory capacity, a quarterly honorarium of £16 13s. 4d. for his services—£66 13s. 4d. per annum. A curious sum!

The years were going on; times were changing, and by the end of 1910, eight years after the first announcement of "garrage", the Directors decided to add to the accommodation for motor cars.

The ladies of the Meikle family began to appear at the Company's annual meetings, and even to submit and second motions. These meetings during the first 60 years of the Company's existence had been held in the Goold Halls at 5 St. Andrew Square, Edinburgh, a practice which continued right down to the General Strike of 1926, when the Chairman, Dr Gordon Meikle, thought it advisable to alter the arrangements and hold the annual general meeting in Strathearn House, as the Hydro is still called in formal moments. The following year the Board decided that the A.G.M. should be at the Hydro once again, and that move has held ever since.

For many years the Company had turned envious eyes on the Knock and other lands belonging to Ferntower Estate, but they had never had an opportunity to acquire them. 1912 was to be the year, however. The proprietor was Lord Abercromby, and he wished to sell the whole estate consisting of three areas. Difficulty in doing so brought about the decision to sell in lots and the Hydro Company purchased all of Ferntower Estate to the north of the Perth road, extending to 423 acres, for £12,000, entering into possession on 11th November 1912. Four months later Dr Meikle, founder of this remarkable Establishment, died, aged 79. The borrowing powers of the Company had already been raised from £25,000 to £35,000, and Dr Meikle's scheme for presenting the Knock of Crieff to the town was known, though not effected. Dr Gordon, who was appointed to succeed his father in all his offices, carried through those intentions. At almost the same time the Memorandum of the Company was amended, and it was agreed that Mr George L. Duncan, a son-in-law of Dr Meikle, should assist the Chairman in the management of the business.

Mr Duncan, who had married Miss Bessie Mackay Meikle, took up his duties at a most opportune moment, for when the First World War broke out he proved an invaluable colleague taking over from Dr Gordon all the extra work created by new regulations dealing with the war-time situation.

Despite the effect the war must have had on the Establishment, the word "war" does not appear in the minutes until the 18th of May 1917, when a request came from Crieff Golf Club to allow the old lease held by them for the course on the Knock to lapse, as that course was being discontinued and closed owing to the war.

How different were those war years to the years 1939–45! The Hydro was not commandeered. The daily average of visitors did not decline. It rose—1915, 163; 1916, 187; 1917, 187·5; 1918, 186; 1919, 217. Difficulties consisted mainly of coping with food rationing and the call-up of staff, but thanks to Mr Duncan these things were tackled with resolution and precision and overcome successfully.

Towards the end of the war Dr Gordon Meikle intimated his resignation as Secretary of the Company and moved that Mr Duncan be appointed. This was approved, and at the same time he became a Director. He occupied the Overdale villa as one of his emoluments, shortly afterwards moving to Strathearn Leigh, as Dr Gordon was then living in Dalmhor.

Mrs Agnes Meikle had died and her estate was being wound up, meaning that Dalmhor would come on the market if the Company did not buy it. The Directors felt it advisable to purchase it and did so for £1,900, with the condition that if any member of the Meikle family desired to repurchase at any time they could do so at the same price. The main entrance to the Hydro passed through the Dalmhor feu which extended on both sides of Ewanfield road.

By 1921 the farm of Culcrieff, adjoining the Hydro grounds, had been bought for £3515. There were about 150 acres arable and 50 acres woodlands, the growing timber being valued at about £900, and it had a good dwelling house and steading, easily adapted for dairying. Before this happened Mr Duncan had started rearing hens at Ferntower because of "the present high cost of eggs".

The building valuation of the House itself for fire insurance stood at £174,000 at this time. Two years later (1925) extensive fire precautions were taken. Alarms were installed and another iron stair built, for the chapel (east) wing this time, so that, considering all that had been done the insurance company reduced the premiums by six per cent. In view of all these precautions an unusual situation arose in 1933. Apparently the Secretary for Scotland wrote to the Local Authority saying—I quote the minute—

". . . . . it had been reported to him (by whom was not stated) that the facilities for escape in the Hydropathic in case of fire were inadequate."

He asked them to look into this.

"A deputation from the Town Council called at the Hydropathic and satisfied themselves that our precautions were sufficient, but our Chairman decided to obtain advice of Messrs. Merryweather and Sons. Ltd., London, and proposals with plans, estimates, got from Mills and Shepherd, Dundee, were put in hand for completion before Christmas. Total cost £636 9s. 6d."

The whole field of insurance was gone into at the same time as the Company succeeded in having the premium reduced, and one aspect which arose received special mention, thus—

"*Public liability and Third Party risks.* There were certain reservations (in the policy) regarding the 'treatment' of visitors which did not and do not fully meet our requirements in view of the peculiar circumstances in which we stand as a Hydropathic. Draft policy to be submitted to meet our requirements."

As the years passed by, a shortage of garage accommodation was noted and more lock-ups provided from time to time. A motor 'bus caught the attention of the Board and ultimately made its appearance—"A great novelty and a great event" is how Miss Ewing, hostess for many years, described its arrival. As stated, efforts were being made to find covered space for the cars that kept arriving with visitors, but with the coming of the 'Thirties this became obviously impossible and many people had to leave their vehicles on the sides of the forecourt; and now (1967) when about 98 per cent. of the guests bring cars a new parking space has been made above the boiler house to the east of the main entrance, and the last bend at the top of the main drive has been straightened out. And continuing the motor car saga, two petrol pumps, each with a 500 gallon tank were installed at the garage in 1927. The following year a 30 cwt. tipping waggon to take the place of the horses and carts that brought coal up from the station, and a car for hiring were bought.

Another problem that kept pace with the development of the business was the provision of houses for employees. As early as 1923 cottages at Dallerie, for laundry workers, had been erected, using concrete blocks, and the dwelling house there was later divided into flats. In 1930 a house was built, with Government subsidy, to replace the Blue Gate lodge. Now the Company owns over thirty houses, three of which have been built in the last five years.

Eighty years ago an old lady who came regularly to the Hydropathic from Glasgow declared "I never come here but I find Dr Meikle in the mortar tub". That, in simple language, means that alterations and additions seem to be "built in" to the constitution just as much as the original bricks and mortar.

I mentioned that the ladies of the Meikle family had begun to take an active part in the annual meetings of the Company. In January Dr Gordon proposed that Miss Marjory Jane Meikle (one of his sisters) should be made a Director; Dr Hunter seconded the proposal and it was approved. The lengthy task of converting certain bedrooms into bathrooms and of putting hot and cold water into the bedrooms occupied the first few years of the 'Thirties. This was a period of "slump" in business; so much so that the Chairman stated that he and the Secretary (Mr Duncan) had voluntarily accepted a five per cent. cut in their salaries as from 1st December 1931. Income was down by £5298 because there had been fewer visitors. The ten shillings per share bonus in addition to the dividend, the Directors decided, should not be paid this year, a situation which held until 1937, when it was restored, by reason of the numbers of visitors rising to something like the heights of the second half of the 1920s. That interim period, besides containing low numbers of arrivals, also saw high figures of expenditure. Putting hot and cold water in 172 bedrooms had cost well over £4000 while upkeep and repairs on the fabric of the main part of the House, plus a new Pelton wheel for the generating station came to £1660 in 1935. The larger sum was spread over a few years. In 1935, also, Mr H. A. Walker, who was a Director at this time, proposed that the voluntary cuts in the Chairman's and the Secretary's salaries should be restored, and this was agreed. In the summer of that same year the Rev. Dr Joseph Leckie, Cupar, Fife, who had been a Director since 1910, died, and at the November meeting the Directors unanimously agreed to ask Dr Joseph Primrose Leckie, his older son, to take his father's place on the Board.

The Town Council of Crieff, having now responsibility for the Knock, decided to build a path up to the indicator which had been placed on the summit in 1930 in memory of Mr Robert Rule of Crieff, so the Company gave a donation of £20 towards this object—not the first time the Meikle family had been engaged in such a public-spirited action. At the height of post-war unemployment and in the depth of the trade depression in 1920–21, Mrs George L. Duncan, to mitigate the hardships of people in the town, generously employed men in the upkeep of the Jubilee Walk on the Knock. Much earlier than this Lady Baird, of Ferntower, had "The Green Walk" made round the Knock to relieve the destitution of the weavers in Crieff, paying them one shilling and a loaf of bread per day.

A threat to feu some 16½ acres lying along the cinder path to the west of the Hydro brought the Directors into action promptly, the Chairman being instructed to come to the best terms possible with the Drummond Estates, owners of the ground, who proposed a price of £1200.

Some idea of the multifarious duties of the Manager and his Secretary may be glimpsed by looking at a list of capital charges in 1937. Here it is:

Work on Barvick Cottage. H. and c. installation. Tomato house. Lock-ups. Laundry transformer. Steam heating in Chapel wing. Land on Knock—legal charges. Indoor brooders. Hoe cultivator. Armature. Summer house at Overdale. Boiling pan for pigs' food. Filing cabinet.

I tried, earlier in this chapter, to stress the catholicity of the Manager's job in which he literally deals with everything, from a needle to an anchor. That is no exaggeration, for the Hydro includes, as well as joiners', plumbers' and electricians premises, an upholstery workshop, a sewing room and several boats on Loch Earn. George Duncan, a man of sterling quality, came very much into this picture and took a great deal off the shoulders of Dr Gordon. In fact, the Doctor spoke to the Board about getting Mr A. W. Duncan to assist his brother, and it was left to the Chairman to arrange. Alex Duncan came on to the staff in the spring of 1937, and a measure of the character of his brother was shown at that time, and again in November of that year. He agreed to relinquish £300 of his own salary to help to pay that of his brother. Then in November, the Chairman "regretted having to inform the Directors that the Cashier, who had been with them for many years, had admitted embezzlement". The auditor explained that the amount was over £700 but the Cashier had returned £300. Though the system of bookkeeping incorporated an efficient check, the fraud had been carefully planned and taken advantage of Mr Duncan's absence, through illness, and a number of office staff changes.

Although I can conceive of no grounds on which the Manager could be regarded as having any responsibility for the Company's loss, [the auditor continued], Mr Duncan had, immediately the deficiency was confirmed at £436, paid that sum to the credit of the Company's bank account.

The Board expressed appreciation of Mr Duncan's generous action. After consideration of all the circumstances it was decided not to take any steps to prosecute the cashier.

With the summer of 1938 the war clouds over Europe had grown darker, a threat which was reflected in the minutes of November, when the appointment of wardens in connection with Crieff air raid precautions was reported. Trouble, how great few imagined, lay ahead.

RATES, RULES, REGULATIONS

"The terms were extremely moderate, and the organisation, service and comfort (without rank luxury) were mechanically perfect."

J. J. BELL

Before plunging into the war-time gloom let us look again at the Hydro regime.

The bells mentioned by J. J. Bell and Mrs Charles really were an outstanding feature of life in Strathearn House. Where the glass doors from the ground floor corridor lead into the dining-room to-day, there was a shallow recess in the wall with doors shutting it off, and it was inside this recess that there hung the various ropes which, when pulled, sounded the bells all over the building. Two persons who remember the carillon being rung have each described the action of the ringer as "like milking a cow".

Each bell—gong might, perhaps, be a better word to describe their shape and action—looked like an inverted saucer and measured about ten or twelve inches across, and all sounded different notes. The tongue or clapper was not suspended inside the gong but rose from below and struck it when the rope was pulled on the ground floor. It was a very pleasing sound. As there were a number of ropes to be pulled the gongs did not all sound at the same time but in rotation, at the will of the person working the ropes, and each rope was pulled several times thus producing a delightful sustained harmony (unless when one bell was cracked).

It was a most ingenious idea and might still have been in operation had not the military forces in the Hydro during the war destroyed the system, which was too expensive to replace.

Before the bells began to ring, "big Ben" in the tower had sounded a warning to bring guests in from the town, the golf course and the grounds. So far as I can ascertain, the tower bell rang quarter of an hour before breakfast and lunch, and half an hour before dinner. The times of these meals were generally 8.30 a.m., 1.15 p.m. and 7 p.m. In winter breakfast was at 9 o'clock.

A prospectus marked in pencil, "May 1915", gives these times and is a most interesting document well worth examining, though it is doubtful if the pencil marking is correct, for the name "Gleneagles" is used as one of the railway junctions when, in fact, the station was "Crieff Junction" at that time.

First, the weekly terms charged when the Hydropathic opened its doors on 7th August 1868. At the very first annual general meeting of the Company in April 1868, it was decided that the charges should be "Not less than £2 9s. per week or 7s. 6d. per day—a higher rate for superior rooms and a lower rate where two persons occupied the same bedroom." Those terms lasted for four years and then, on account of "the increased cost of Food, and all other expences, it would be proper that the ordinary charge to single visitors should be raised in July 1872, from 7s. 6d. a day (or £2 12s. 6d. per week) to 8s. a day (or £2 16s. per week); for two persons occupying one room, from £4 11s. to £4 14s. 6d.; for one person with a child from £3 13s. 6d. to £3 17s. per week. The age of children admissible and the charges for superior rooms, fires, special service, etc., to remain as at present." Later that same year the rates authorised were, "for the months of July, August and September, £3 3s. for each visitor; £2 16s. for spring and autumn months; and £2 9s. per week for winter; rates for children and servants to be raised as resolved in former minutes".

As already noted in the Court case of 1881, children under six years were not admitted, but it seems likely, from the two references to children in 1872 that some similar rule was in force from the opening day. Modern times, modern manners, and to-day there is no limit to the age of visitors—at either end of life's span.

One of the sights of the Hydro during June, July and August is the nursery, where so many toddlers begin to acquire the habit of holidaying there. The companionship, the toys and playroom equipment, the spacious grounds

with paddling pool, swings and so on, the meals together—
all combine to give those little people a sense of belonging,
and if not of actual memories, at least of vague recollections
of new friends, new games and fun.

Modern developments in the nursery have arisen directly
from the ideas put forward and the routine established by
"Nanna"—she was the Leckie children's nurse for many
years—and backed up by Dr Joe Leckie. Nanna was a
familiar figure for ten post-war years, with her nurses' cap
and her strong but kindly personality.

As stated above, children under ten years have all their
meals in their own dining room beside the nursery, a regula-
tion which brings ease and relief to young mothers, and
helps to make their stay at the Hydro a much more restful
holiday. I recall making the acquaintance of a young
couple and not knowing for several days that they had three
children with them. They said the children were always
clamouring in the early morning to get out to play; always
had something to do. The days were not long enough.

Of course, there have always existed special terms for
children, and in the 1915 prospectus are these lines:

Children under twelve having meals in the Nursery	£1 15s.
During July, August, September, Xmas, New Year	
and Easter holidays	£2 2s.

Children having meals in the main dining room were, and
are charged as adults.

For the ordinary visitor in 1915 the charges in the high
season were £3 10s. per week and £3 3s. where two or three
shared the same bedroom. In March, April, May, June, and
October the terms were £3 3s. and £2 16s.; and in November,
December, January and February—Christmas, New Year
and Easter excluded—they dropped to £2 16s. and £2 9s.

Here let us "pause and consider"—like Para Handy. I
mentioned the terms at the Hydro in 1868 and 1872.
Compare them with those charged in 1915, over forty years
later, and what do we find? We find that a married couple,
or two persons sharing the same room, could stay at the
Hydropathic for exactly the same expenditure in 1915 as in

1872—£3 3s., £2 16s., and £2 9s. in high, mid and low seasons respectively. Surely this is a record for restraint and good management.

⸱For a coal fire in your bedroom, from 1s. 6d. per day was charged, and 9d. if only for the evening, while 6d. extra secured you breakfast in bed—or any other meal in a private room.

Private servants sharing visitors' rooms were rated at £2 2s. and £1 15s., according to the season, but if they had to have a single room then the rate was £1 1s. and 17s. 6d. more, respectively.

"Accommodation for Private Horses, Carriages and Motors (Inspection Pit)." Dogs were forbidden in the House (and still are), but could be kept at the stables for 2s. 6d. a week. That figure is now 1s. a day. The prospectus goes on:

> During July, August and September, accommodation should be secured before coming, definitely stating length of stay.

This request for a definite assurance of the length of stay was actually an echo from the past. In October 1896, nearly thirty years after commencing business, the Manager reported

> . . . that the number requiring single rooms, and the neglect to give notice of departure, made it very difficult to accommodate visitors who wished to come, and may necessitate some additional notice as to engaging rooms for a specific period.

Just a year later the Chairman (Dr Thomas Meikle) reported that a considerable effort had been made to get visitors to intimate the duration of their visit by using slips but it was only partially successful. The slips were in these terms:

> Owing to the number of applications, and the difficulty in arranging for the succession of Visitors during July, August and September, intending Visitors require to take their rooms for a definite period.

It took the Management many, many years to persuade visitors to state just how long they intended to stay—a measure, surely, of the pace of life at that time, and also of the calibre of those persons frequenting the Hydropathic then. This attitude can be understood when one recalls the fact that most couples and families of Victorian and Edwardian days were not prepared to tear themselves from their smooth and stately routine at home, unless for some very worthwhile reason. It was the usual thing to move to coast or country for *at least* a month, and two months or three was not uncommon. The husbands, having had their "fling" of a fortnight or so, would then travel to business daily, the train service in those days being more frequent and faster than we have known it for a long time. Glasgow and Edinburgh were the daily destination of quite a number of men living at the Hydro with wives and families for the summer months. If the weather proved genial towards the end of their stay, why then, they would simply remain at the Hydro for another two or three weeks. Customers like these really posed a problem, for they could not lightly be turned out. Nowadays no one would dream of going without giving a firm date for leaving.

Medical attention cost 10s. 6d. for the first consultation and there was also available electric and massage treatment at moderate charges. No gratuities were to be given, the staff at this period receiving a bonus yearly from the Directors. Instructions about "lights out" were included in the prospectus which said:

Lights off Public Rooms at 10.30 p.m.; lowered in Winter Gardens at 11 p.m.; Bedrooms at 11.15 p.m.

These times were repeated in the prospectus for 1921, a also were the details of

Family Worship after Breakfast, and 9.45 p.m.
Sundays, 9 p.m.

The descriptive matter in the brochure about the House is well worth quoting. Here it is:

STRATHEARN HYDROPATHIC ESTABLISHMENT
COMPANY, LIMITED

This Establishment occupies a most advantageous site, in a district of great natural and historical interest, selected by

Dr Meikle from many others in Scotland on account of the salubrity of its climate, and the varied attractiveness of its scenery. Many testimonies to the healthiness and beauty of the situation might be cited. The *Gazetteer of Scotland* says:— "Crieff is famous for the salubrity of its climate, its sheltered site, pure air, excellent water, and freedom from epidemics; and hence has long been esteemed 'the Montpelier of Scotland,' and is a favourite for invalids in quest of health." John Brown, M.D., in his *Horae Subsecivae*, remarks that, "There is not in all Scotland, or as far as I have seen in all else, a more exquisite twelve miles of scenery than that between Crieff and the foot of Lochearn." Charles Reade, the eminent novelist, in his published Memoirs, states:— "The habitable globe possesses no more delightful spot than Crieff."

Strathearn House, 440 feet above sea-level, surrounded by extensive grounds of 40 acres, stands on a commanding plateau, about a mile from the Railway Station, mid-way up the southern slope, and sheltered by the 'Knock of Crieff', a wooded hill (of Old Red Sandstone) which rises to a height of 900 feet. The view is unequalled, including the extensive and picturesque valley of the Earn, with the mountain ranges beyond, seen extending over a distance of 50 miles. The places of interest are easily reached by excellent roads, which lead through some of the most charming landscapes in Scotland. In the immediate vicinity of the House are excellent walks. For further information, see District Map.

The House has been carefully arranged with a view to the health and comfort of Visitors. The Public Rooms, including a Lounge or Winter Garden, are lofty and commodious, the Bedrooms are large and comfortable. The whole building is lit by Electricity, and thoroughly ventilated, and warmed by a well-adapted heating apparatus. The Bathing arrangements, carried out by experienced and skilled attendants, are of the most complete and modern description, including Turkish, Swimming, Electric and other Baths; Electricity, in "High Frequency", and other forms being also used. The cure of the suffering and exhausted is specially aimed at. There is an abundant supply of the purest water. There is a lift for Visitors.

Besides Croquet and Tennis lawns within the grounds there are two good Golf Courses, of 18 and 9 holes, within five minutes' walk.

N.B.—Passengers to Crieff from the South sometimes change carriages at Gleneagles. Those North and East of Perth generally come *via* Methven Junction.   Visitors will secure the Company's Omnibus, on their arrival at Crieff, by informing the Station-Master or Ticket-Collector at Gleneagles, or (when coming *via* Methven Junction) the Guard at Perth, who will telegraph, without charge, the number wishing it.   'Bus fares, 1s. each; Members of one Family, 9d. each.

Resident Physician, T. Gordon Meikle, M.B. C.M.

The substitution of "Gleneagles" for "Crieff Junction" shows that the leaflet was revised after 1915, but most of it must have been written much earlier.   The narrative of the "Prominent New York State Club Woman" shows suspicious similarity with a number of the phrases in the prospectus, and the reference to Dr Meikle (the founder) in the second line of the prospectus makes no distinction between him and Dr T. Gordon Meikle, the Resident Physician, who was his son.   Dr Thomas Henry Meikle, had, in fact, been dead two years before this brochure was printed, and on looking at prospectuses for 1919 and 1921 it was not until the latter year that the words "the late Dr Meikle" were inserted.   Further, there is no mention in any other material that has come to light except the very earliest prospectuses that Dr Meikle selected Crieff district "from many others in Scotland". That phrase alone makes one think that this text was probably written by Dr Meikle himself.   It would be of great interest to learn, more than a hundred years after, the names of those other places which the Doctor considered before fixing on Crieff.

I have referred to the prospectus of 1921 and may say that it is exactly the same as the earlier one except for two or three very minor changes.   "Supper" at 8.30 o'clock on Sunday evenings has become "Dinner" at 8 o'clock, in the later edition.   Which again recalls a vexed question of April 1887, when Dr Meikle was so exercised about the time at which "Dinner" should be served that he consulted the Directors.

The Manager laid before the meeting statistics (and prospectuses) of 29 other Hydropathic Establishments, with special reference to early and late dinners, from which it appeared that 13 had dinner from 1 to 2 o'clock and 16 had dinner from 6 to 7 o'clock. The Directors agreed to the experiment of a late dinner being tried during the summer months.

So runs the minute, but it does not state what was served instead of dinner in the middle of the day.

But the emancipation of the younger people wrought by the First World War had little effect on the routine of the Hydro, for, if this 1921 prospectus is to be believed, lights still were doused at 10.30 p.m. in the public rooms and lowered in bedrooms at 11.15, a practice which continued into the 1930s. By this date, also, there was only one golf course in the town—on the Hydropathic Company's ground below Ferntower, where it has remained since it was made in 1914–15 and improved in 1924–25 on suggestions by James Braid.

By the end of the First World War the weekly terms had had to be increased, and the 1919 prospectus shows them as being £4 7s. 6d. for single room, £4 os. 6d. for a double, in the high seasons and holidays; £4 os. 6d. single, and £3 13s. 6d. double, in March, April, May and October; and £3 13s. 6d. and £3 os. 6d. respectively in November, December, January and February. Terms for children were proportionately raised.

Having once begun to put up prices, it was found difficult to stop, for the economics of the post-war period called the tune. These 1919 figures were all increased for the 1920 brochure, 7s. being added to each individual classification.

Further changes took place when the 1921 brochure was made up for June of that year. It had been decided, apparently, that the "Mid-season" terms should be done away with, for the details simply give July, August, September, Christmas, New Year and Easter Holidays £5 8s. 6d. (single) and £5 1s. 6d. (double), and for the rest of the 12 months £5 1s. 6d. and £4 14s. 6d.

One other change in the regulations is of interest:

Children not allowed in Public Rooms except with Guardians.

The upward trend in charges, begun in 1919, slowed down considerably after that and despite the radical change in the public attitude to money, following the Second World War, (during which the Hydro was occupied by troops), we find in a folder entitled "Re-opening Notice" that the terms over most of the year were £6 6s. to £8 8s. per week, while the high season—it was now June to the end of September—and holidays went to £7 7s. and £9 9s. This, it has to be stressed, included breakfast, luncheon (with biscuits and cheese), afternoon tea, dinner (with savoury and coffee to follow), bedroom, baths, dancing, tennis, putting green, croquet lawn, table tennis, swimming pool, and, for a very small fee, billiards. Throughout the years the Directors of the Company have *never* allowed to creep in that insidious policy of "extras"—items that most people do not expect to be included in the weekly terms; for example, coffee after dinner; afternoon teas; baths, and so on. Extra charges are made for gas fires in bedrooms, and this is an excellent arrangement, for many people still like to sleep in a cool room, not affected by central heating, and so do not pay for what they do not use.

The corridors, of course, are always warm, as are the public rooms. Indeed, on sunny days of spring and autumn the Winter Garden can become too warm—surely a much more cheerful fault than too cold.

In recent years the tariff has had to be raised several times, owing to rising costs; to meet, for example, the penalties imposed by the Selective Employment Tax, so that the rates are now, on average eleven guineas in the low season and seventeen guineas in the high season.

WAR—AND AFTER

"I saw the lightning's gleaming rod
Reach forth and write upon the sky . . ."

JOAQUIN MILLER

The writing was in the sky, most certainly. As the months of 1939 passed the gloom thickened, and the daunting thought that the Hydropathic might be requisitioned sprang up. On 18th September, 15 days after war was declared, a special meeting of Directors considered the implications. They were told by Dr Gordon that he and the Secretary had seen several Army officers all of whom were of opinion that both the Hydro and Ferntower would be needed for billeting troops. The Chairman said he had pointed out to Scottish Command certain facts which rendered the Establishment unsuitable for such purpose, and he submitted a copy of his memorandum, which was approved. He was authorised to take any further action he thought advisable to prevent, if possible, the Hydropathic being taken over for the billeting of troops. This war was not going to be like the last.

That memorandum, dated 16th September 1939, produced nothing but a polite acknowledgement. Then the blow fell. Only a matter of days after receiving that acknowledgement, notices commandeering the Hydropathic and Ferntower House were served on the Company. At 8 p.m. on Friday, 6th October 1939, these notices were handed to Dr Gordon. On Monday, 9th October, only three days later and a week earlier than had been suggested by verbal message, troops marched into Ferntower. Barely a week later and the Hydropathic itself was subjected to a similar invasion. Barely a week in which to remove most of the goods and chattels in a house with 188 bedrooms, huge public rooms and ancillary apartments. Where could all the furniture be stored with some hope of it remaining dry and in fairly good condition for an indefinite number of years? Fortunately, as stated previously, part of the stables had been converted into garages and many more lock-ups added, a good many of them with heated pipes running through. These, then, made up the hibernation quarters for the furniture. Again, fortunately, and thanks to the foresight of the Chairman and Secretary, steps had been taken in advance to get reports from Messrs. Mills and Shepherd, architects, Dundee, and Messrs. Morrison and McChlery, valuers, Glasgow, on the conditions of the building and of the chattels, many of which were taken over by the Army. "No attempt," said Dr Meikle, "was made to give us a 'Marching-in' report, and Ferntower House was relinquished without a 'Marching-out' report."

All employees not actually required for the maintenance of the Establishment had been discharged and a claim for compensation in respect of these notices was included in the main claim. The question of the managerial staff salaries had to be left over until there was some indication of the line the Government were going to adopt in that matter. The minutes go on:

"It was noted that the Chairman, the Secretary, Mr A. W Duncan and Mr Swanston Drysdale did not draw their salaries for last quarter to 1st March 1940."

One source of revenue in which the Directors were led "up the garden path" was the use to be made of the laundry. One of the Regimental Quartermasters calculated that there would be about 1,000 men getting their washing done at Dallerie laundry; or work to the extent of approximately £35 to £40 per week. Actually, the receipts never reached half of that.

As might have been expected, the international situation had seriously affected the numbers of visitors throughout a large part of the season, and from the day the requisition notice was served until Easter of 1949—ten years all but six months—the business of the Hydropathic as a hydropathic was completely quiescent. Luckily other sections of the business of the Company went on—the farm, the estate, the laundry, all contributed something towards income and required the administration of the Chairman and the Secretary, assisted by Mr Alex Duncan.

A note of somewhat grim amusement was sounded by the notorious "Lord Haw-Haw", who broadcast from Germany that troops had been billeted in Crieff Hydro.

A few of the male employees had been kept on, among them Mr Douglas McLennan, and he recalls some of the scenes and some of the scares of those days.

"The Signals and Engineers came first and the NAAFI occupied the Winter Garden. The Drawing room was the officers' club. The troops trained in the country round about and a rifle range was established at Ferntower. I was taken over by the Army and tried my best to look after the building, but the soldiers set fire to parts of it now and again. I remember being called out three times in a week to put out fires. Later in the war we had Polish troops billeted here and it was a year after the war was over before they left. A lot of damage had been done by that time—seven or eight years as Army billets."

The Company's auditor at this time was Mr A. C. Chalmers, a senior member of the firm of John E. Watson and Macharg, C.A., Glasgow, and he had a busy time keeping track of all the facilities and items that the Army took over from the Hydro. For example, by May 1940, he explained to the Board the various claims lodged under the Compensation (Defence) Act of 1939. They covered the rent of the Hydropathic, Ferntower and the electric plant; the price of chattels taken over; the wages of staff dismissed; expenses of moving furniture, air raid precautions, insurance and professional fees; storing of furniture; rent for 20 lock-ups; petrol pump hired at 10s. per week; and supply of electric light. An immediate payment to account had been asked, but no response was received for some time.

Pending settlement of compensation, the Chairman suggested that the salaries of himself, Mr G. L. Duncan and Mr A. W. Duncan should be reduced by 50 per cent. as from 1st March 1940, and this was approved.

A deal with Messrs. Peter McAinsh for timber on part of the Knock took place, the price paid being £1800, while a request by the Golf Club for a reduction in rent was met by a rebate of £15 each half year on condition that the rent was paid on the date due.

On the advice of the auditor the Company decided that no dividend could be paid. Compensation claims were substantial, he pointed out, but the ultimate result of these seemed uncertain. This decision affected the servants' deposits—more is said about them elsewhere—and the Directors resolved to credit that account with interest at four per cent. The question of letting vacant staff houses arose and the Chairman and Secretary were left to settle it.

At the 73rd annual general meeting of the Company on 24th May 1940, the Chairman said:

"We meet at a time of crisis in the history of the world and at this hour it is right that every individual, company and institution in the country should render every assistance within its power to the National cause.

"Your Company was early affected by the outbreak of hostilities as the Hydropathic was requisitioned by the Government on 6th October last and was immediately occupied by the Military Authorities. The normal business of the Company, in consequence, came to a complete standstill, and while the Company possesses extensive assets which do not come under the requisition, these assets have been in the past acquired and maintained in connection with the Hydropathic business and their upkeep now forms a heavy charge on the Company's resources.

"The Directors have taken all steps necessary in connection with the preparation and submission of claims for compensation to the Government, but up to the present time it is not known on what basis compensation will be paid. Since the completion of the Directors' report a payment of £2,000 to account of your Company's claims has been received, but this item cannot be taken in any way as a measure of the amount which will ultimately be paid.

"In view of the uncertainty with regard to compensation, the Directors, after careful consideration, decided with regret that they could not recommend the payment of a dividend at this time. It is hoped that the conditions which presently exist will soon pass and that the shareholders may look forward with confidence to the future of the Company.

Twelve months later it was reported that agreement had been reached as to compensation for the requisition of the Hydro, Ferntower and the garages. The Government were to pay £7,500 per annum as rent and allowances for storage of furniture. A number of smaller claims had not been settled. The salaries of Dr Meikle and Mr Duncan represented three-quarters of those of the previous year, and all other salaries of staff retained had been paid in full. No rents had been collected for houses previously occupied by employees who were dismissed. A dividend of ten per cent. less tax was paid.

The farm was paying handsomely and the laundry also making a profit. By the date of the 1942 A.G.M., however, the Board reached several decisions of note: they would repay all the servants' deposits with the Company, thus ending a scheme which had been going since 1883; they would conserve the resources of the Company for the day when peace would be restored and the Hydropathic again put to the use for which it was intended; they would pay a dividend of five per cent. less Income Tax at 10s. in the £1.

The Chairman, at this meeting made reference to Miss Marjory Meikle, his sister, who had died on 22nd September 1941. She attended her first general meeting in 1909 and became a Director—the first woman to achieve this distinction—in January 1929. Her sister, Mrs Bessie Duncan, had died in 1935, and Miss Margaret Meikle in 1916, in Glasgow. Mrs Edith Meikle had not yet come on to the Board.

The war went on. Much routine work had to be undertaken as well as the solving of war-time problems by empiric, sometimes peremptory methods. All this took its toll of Gordon Meikle and George Duncan. The Doctor was now almost 80 and in the four years of war had led a busy and harassing life. It was not altogether surprising, therefore, when in the spring of 1944 he became ill and passed away on 29th June at Dalmhor, his sister Edith being with him at the end.

For almost 60 years Gordon Meikle had worked for the Strathearn Hydropathic. He first became a Director in

1890, resigned in 1892 in favour of his father, and then in 1904 succeeded William Meikle on the Board when he retired, aged 89. In 1913, on the death of his father, he was appointed Chairman and this office he held till his death.

Mr Duncan was asked to carry on as Managing Director till the annual meeting but before that event, he, too, had gone to his long rest. Like his brother-in-law, he had given faithful service for over 30 years to the Company.

Should the Company carry on the business as before requisition? Or—Should the business be sold? These two questions exercised the minds of the Board at a meeting on 17th June 1945.

The feeling of the Directors seemed to be that the business should be carried on after de-requisition on the lines embodying the principles laid down by the late Dr Thomas H. Meikle and by the late Dr T. Gordon Meikle.

When that sentence was written little did the Directors know what a struggle there would be to set the Establishment edging forward towards widespread custom and the general appreciation of thousands of war-weary folk. For it took four years—a long period of wear and tear on patience and nerves—getting the Polish troops out, rehabilitating the whole House and grounds, and grinding day after day at the almost endless task of obtaining compensation for damage done.

In command of the Company in this very big exercise the Directors placed Dr Joseph P. Leckie, who at that time was in general practice in the Morningside district of Edinburgh. Mr A. W. Duncan became interim secretary.

The fever of change started with decisions on selling or keeping Ferntower House, Overdale, and then Dalmhor; the first two to be kept and Dalmhor to be sold when Mrs Mary Meikle, Dr Gordon's widow, gave it up. Ultimately it went to Morrison's Academy Boarding House Association, in 1946.

"In the near future" was the phrase used by the War Department when asked about the release of the Hydropathic. That was at the beginning of 1946, it took practically a year for this to happen; but once possession of the whole Establishment was regained the pace quickened until, with a re-opening date announced for April 1949, the mountain of work involving all departments seemed insuperable. The Chef, Mr Alexander MacGregor, describes his baptism of work at the Hydro in 1949:

"The day I came for an interview two months before opening, I had to climb over piles of rubble and under scaffolding. Mr Leckie sat in his temporary office with his duffle coat on, surrounded by a sea of plans, and picks, shovels and gum boots. The first three months were trying, to say the least, but at the same time a challenge. Of some eight or nine pieces of equipment, only one gas stove was in operation and sixteen tradesmen including plasterers, plumbers and fitters were working above, below and around us in the kitchen. As the fitters opened steam pipes to make new connections, water cascaded from above and work benches had to be hurriedly shifted. We managed somehow to feed and keep reasonably happy some 150 guests.

"The crowning blow was the discovery a week before opening that there were no curtains for any bedrooms. Dyed hessian was all that was available and this was hastily run up by a local tailor."

The man who bore the brunt of that battle over the months from May 1948, onwards was Mr W. Gordon Leckie, younger brother of the Chairman, who gave him tremendous backing in his efforts to get the House in order for the opening. On the 9th March 1948, the Directors placed on record the appointment of Mr Gordon Leckie, O.B.E., B.Sc., as Managing Director of the Company, to take effect on 1st June 1948.

Details of Mr Leckie's career are given in another chapter, so it is sufficient to say here that he threw himself, heart and soul, into the business of the Hydro though conditions at that time must have been such as to frighten anyone.

During its occupation by the soldiers the interior of the Hydro had been badly wrecked. Licences for rehabilitation work were required at the time, and the official responsible for issuing them told one of the present Directors that the damage in the building was so severe that it presented him with the most difficult problem that he had to face in the whole of Scotland. The claim for damages was of the order of £50,000. To quote Dr Leckie in his statement as Chairman at the A.G.M. in May, 1948:

"In the opinion of the architect [Mr Morrison] and of the Board, the kitchens had to be reconstructed, and the architect was strongly opposed to any attempt to repair the staircases because, in his view, these were so badly worn as to be incapable of this line of treatment. The Board, therefore, were not in a position to apply merely for a licence to make good any damage done by the War Department. Indeed, in the opinion of the Board, this was a Heaven-sent opportunity to undertake essential reconstruction and modernisation. . . .

"We have received information by telephone that we will be granted a licence for £28,500 to proceed with the work on the basement, ground floor and 'new wing', this work to commence sometime in August. A supplementary licence to complete work on the first floor will be applied for shortly. It is proposed to proceed with the provision of bathrooms as planned—the difficulty of finding the necessary iron piping will, doubtless, be overcome. The number of bedrooms available for guests, were the house in full commission, is 180. We hope to open by April 1949, using the East basement and present 'isolation' block; the bedrooms under the Winter Garden, the whole of the 'new wing' and ground floor—78 bedrooms in all. Simultaneously, work will proceed on the first floor, (48 bedrooms) and, as soon as possible, work on the second floor will be tackled—another 48 bedrooms.

"The Staff will be housed in the East Wing attics. The kitchen staff will find accommodation in the old 'isolation' block. In the opinion of the Board it will be easier and more satisfactory to collect an efficient staff in stages, rather than to try to engage a full staff all at once. When the above has been carried out then will be the time to consider whether to re-condition the attics and convert the present ladies' bathrooms into bedrooms. There are 20 guests bedrooms in the attics and conversion of the ladies' bathrooms would provide six more. It is hoped that the schedule for all this work will be out by mid-August. The delay caused by the preparation of schedules will amount to six weeks but is amply justified by the resulting saving of expense."

Nineteen contracts for work went out, the major amounts being for painting and decorating, £6200 approximately; carpentry, £4025; plasterer, £3804; plumbing, £3706; and kitchen equipment, £3073; and the total, £30,240.

In all this vast amount of planning it is interesting to note that the children were not forgotten. Strathearn Leigh, the house built for Dr Thomas Meikle and his family, had been doing well financially, and it was decided to retain it on its present footing "until such time as the demand for a Children's Hotel could be ascertained". The Leigh had been open, mainly for ministers and their wives, since 1948 as a tentative step towards the re-opening of the Hydro, and this had proved a success.

Changes taking place at the top in May 1949, found Mr A. W. Duncan retiring from the Board. The vacancy was filled by the appointment of the present Chairman, Mr J. R. Donaldson, who is a brother-in-law of Mrs Gordon Leckie, and who has had a long association with the Hydro.

Mr Leckie wanted a resident doctor; also someone who would take charge in the absence of the General Manager. Mrs Edith Meikle agreed and asked if Dr Leckie would take this on, to which the Doctor replied accepting and adding that there was scope in the Hydro for physiotherapy, a facility which would be a notable replacement of hydrotherapy and Turkish baths.

Mrs E. P. Meikle proposed and Mrs Mary Meikle seconded the appointment of Dr Leckie as Managing Director and Resident Doctor, and this was agreed.

At the same meeting the two Mrs Meikles asked that prayers should again be held in the drawing-room at 9.30 each morning. This suggestion found agreement, the matter to be looked at later in the light of experience and attendance. A proposal of this kind seems to indicate that morning prayers had been forgotten in the rush of opening the Hydro again after ten years.

It was not only the Company's larger properties that people wanted to buy or let. To sort out the cottages so that they would all be occupied by employees or pensioners took some time and patience, but none was sold, and the Directors turned down a request to rent Dallerie for mushroom growing.

Despite decisions at two consecutive meetings in mid-1949 not to apply for a liquor licence in the meantime, an application did go forward to the October Licensing Court, but it was turned down. At the 83rd general meeting in June 1949, Dr and Mr Leckie were thanked for all the work they had put into the task of rehabilitation, to which the Chairman replied, "It has been a great pleasure to me to perform the work and to see the old building once more in occupation."

Medical treatment, it was hoped, would be available again in January 1950.

Ferntower House had been a source of trouble for some years and when an expert from Dundee reported that dry rot covered an extensive area and the cost of putting the building into order would be around £15,000, the Board decided to maintain the roof, air the place and get an estimate for demolition. At that time (1950) the rents of flats occupied in Ferntower just about covered rates and taxes.

Representations were later made to the appropriate quarters that the house should be preserved, but without success. The building had deteriorated to a dangerous extent so an estimate was obtained for demolition. However, it proved possible to make arrangements with a Territorial Army detachment of Royal Engineers from the Sheffield and Nottingham areas to demolish the 60-foot tower, as an exercise, and therefore without charge to the Company, and this was done in 1962—to the accompaniment of a storm of protest from one of the Town councillors of Dundee. The officer in charge of the men who did the job considered it an extremely valuable exercise for the men, as opportunities for blowing up a target like Ferntower were few and far between.

Alas! Three months later Ferntower House was designated by the Ministry of Works as a building of special architectural or historic interest and worthy of being preserved. It certainly had historic associations. Bonnie

Prince Charlie spent a night there. The notorious General Johnnie Cope camped in the fields below the house in 1745, and has the distinction of having the sixth hole of the golf course named after him.

For a good many years the estate of Ferntower belonged to General Sir David Baird and Lady Baird. He was the hero of Seringapatam, storming and taking the town in 1799; and she is known for having raised to his memory the granite obelisk on the top of the little hill called Tomachastel, which can be clearly seen from the Hydro, as you look to the west. Sir David Baird—a large portrait of him hangs in the drawing room of the Hydro—took a prominent part in bringing Cleopatra's Needle to this country, so the monument on Tomachastel is a small copy of that Needle, standing over 84 feet high. It was erected in 1832.

The General was a very big man and there is a delightful story about his mother, who, when she heard he had been captured and that, as a prisoner he would be chained to another man, is reported to have said, "God help the puir man that's chained to oor Davie."

Although Ferntower estate did not come into the hands of the Company till Martinmas, 1912, Dr Meikle had been tenant of the house since 1897 and used to spend many of the summer months there. Occasionally he would hold a Directors' meeting at Ferntower and indeed, the last meeting before his death in 1913, was held there on 9th November 1912.

In 1951 the shareholders at the A.G.M. expressed great pleasure at the progress the Company had made; the fact that dividends were being resumed; and at the gratifying reports from visitors on the comforts and the food provided at the Hydro.

Overdale as well as Dalmhor had been sold by this time.

In this year, also, one of the two remaining members of the Meikle family who were Directors of the Company, died —Mrs Edith Meikle—and a tribute to her was paid at the annual meeting in May. She had been a Director for just over six years.

Another sad loss struck the Company early in the following

year (1952), the Chairman, Dr Joseph P. Leckie, dying suddenly in the Royal Infirmary, Perth, where he had been taken for treatment. For nearly eight years he had been Chairman and latterly undertook the duties of Resident Physician, and also Joint Managing Director with his brother, Mr Gordon Leckie.

And here I quote from a letter received from someone who has known Crieff Hydro for a long time.

"It is impossible to overestimate the debt which the Hydro owes to Dr Joseph Leckie, Mr Gordon Leckie, their wives and their families for giving the Hydro a new lease of life after the military occupation. In hotel-keeping they were all amateurs, but they flung themselves into their new task with great zest and great success. They seemed to the visitors to possess inexhaustible energy. No detail escaped them; they laid themselves out to make their customers feel happy and at home. Throughout the day they were constantly in evidence, always making time to chat with visitors, giving small parties especially to those who seemed lonely or friendless, and then dancing every dance with vigour undiminished by a long day's labour. Dr Joe's daughter Barbara, now Mrs Lyon, started country dancing and taught the guests the right way to dance a reel; Gordon's daughter Jean, now Mrs William Leckie, was housekeeper and, to those who were ill, a nurse by both day and night."

The truth of all that will be especially appreciated by those who have spent holidays at the Hydro for some years.

To fill the post of Chairman the Board unanimously appointed Mr J. Reginald Donaldson, and Dr C. G. Strachan and Mr J. A. Milligan were made Directors. Dr Strachan, another whose ties with the Establishment went back a long way, was a brother-in-law of Dr Joe and Mr Gordon, having married Miss Annie Leckie.

The financial position at that period was sound and the volume of business was increasing, so that a growing number of improvements were being suggested and undertaken. It was decided to "dedicate" 20 acres of woodland on the estate—a figure that has now grown to 178 acres. A suggestion for a superannuation scheme came up, and it became a reality a year later. The difficulty of operating a television projector off direct electrical current did not prevent the Manager installing a set for the coronation of Queen Elizabeth in 1953. The 12.30 p.m. 'bus from town to Hydro came into operation.

Dr Strachan's offer of his services as Medical Officer was accepted. The average number of guests staying at the Hydro over twelve months reached a higher level than since 1930, when the figure was 171·5 and the arrivals totalled 7,210; but these totals were nothing like so good as in May 1925, when the daily average reached 195 and the arrivals 7,860. Nowadays, of course, arrivals run into five figures and the daily average is around 250.

Mr Chalmers, the Company's auditor, when asked to explain the relationship between the earning capacity of the Company and the capital employed, thought that the share capital bore little relationship to the capital actually employed, so that the position was rather misleading to those unacquainted with the actual facts.

The Board might consider, therefore, increasing the share capital to, say, £60,000 by issuing three bonus shares for every five shares held, and that the £25 shares should be issued as £1 shares and bring the Company into line with modern practice.

After a full discussion of the position the Board decided, in 1954, to seek authority for the capital to be increased to £75,000 in shares of £1 each, and that £22,500 of the general reserve fund be capitalised by the issue of three bonus shares for every five held. The A.G.M. and extraordinary general meeting both approved of this plan.

A shop for the convenience of visitors was considered, the alcove in the hall being a suitable situation. A Mr Gill, the first tenant of the shop, was asked to sell specified articles, especially newspapers, likely to be needed by visitors.

One problem which the Manager brought to the Board was the number of permanent residents to be accepted. Considerable numbers of elderly persons were asking for permanent and for winter accommodation, but so many regular visitors booked in for Christmas and New Year that the position had to be carefully watched. It was finally agreed that the number should be 32, at the discretion of the Manager. The privilege of permanent residence is deeply appreciated. Residents have shown their gratitude in many different ways. One lady a resident for eight years wrote and illustrated the poem which hangs framed in the front hall.

With higher wages and increases in general costs, the Hydropathic tariff had to go up, but even then, it was pointed out at the time (1956), "Our charges are very moderate as compared with any other comparable establishment." It also appeared that they could not hope for any marked increase in visitors over "the already fantastic numbers shown in the daily average". But still foodstuffs, fuel, rates, taxes and wages went up, and in the next year or two, with numbers of children increasing, the income, because of that, remained steady. The Secretary was authorised to waive the increase in the rates where it would result in hardship for residents.

A hunt took place for a "sick bay" for Hydro patients— if any. Houses in Ferntower Road were inspected and the Establishment premises looked at with this project in mind. Dr Strachan, however, could find no better place than the old isolation block at the east end of the basement floor, which had been occupied by Dr Joe and Mrs Barbara Leckie and retained by her on being appointed hostess, after the death of her husband. Alternative accommodation had to be found for her if these rooms were used for patients. Ultimately, Mrs Leckie moved into Ferntower Cottage, lying to the east of the east drive into the grounds. Dr Strachan, for whom the cottage had been restored, lived there until his death in 1957.

The question of physiotherapy treatment which had been available in the Hydro for many years, led in the end to discussions with the Hospital Board for the area, with a view to amalgamation of the service, but that idea fell through and the Hydro once more has its own physiotherapist, attending on certain days of the week.

More changes occurred in 1957 and 1958 by the deaths of Mrs Mary Meikle—the last of that name on the Board— Dr Strachan, and Mr A. C. Chalmers, who for about 20 years had acted as auditor to the Company. As the Chairman said to the Board, "his interest in the Hydro far exceeded that of accountancy, and his very long association with the Company made his advice of unique value". Tributes to Mrs Meikle and Dr Strachan were also paid at the annual general meeting.

Mr G. L. Barr and Mrs Barbara Leckie became Directors and were welcomed at the 91st A.G.M. in May 1958. There followed at the end of that meeting, an extraordinary general meeting at which the Chairman announced that shareholders would receive one new share for every complete number of four shares held. The Directors felt it their duty to pass on a part of the prosperity of the business to the shareholders and hoped, with continuing prosperity, to maintain the present dividend of 10 per cent.

Another feature pleasing to the Directors was the fact that the holiday seasons were lengthening and they now classed October as a mid-season rather than a low season month.

It seems that at this time records were being broken in various ways—arrivals kept going up; the demand for winter accommodation kept going up but had to be discouraged, say the minutes, as they could not "reduce still further the numbers of our clientele clamouring to get in over the New Year."; and profits, too, kept going up. Expenditure, because of certain moves, was heavy. Nine new rooms were provided in the east end of the basement flat, including the one time "isolation" block. The laundry required a new boiler. But with the season getting longer almost year by year, the staff were having a considerable strain put upon them, working as they did at high pressure for the greater part of the year. To them the Chairman expressed the gratitude of all the shareholders. The bonus to the staff had risen greatly from the £900 voted by the Board in the first year, and it was now about twice that and, if necessary, would go higher.

A small farm of about 40 acres on the south shore of Loch Earn, bought by the Company from the Drummond Estates, was taken over on the 15th May 1957. Trouble with the tenant, however, went on for several years. The banks of the Loch at this point form a well-nigh perfect spot for picnicking on summer afternoons, and from one of the jetties on the beach enterprising or just daft young people can enjoy the pleasures of water ski-ing over or in the none too warm water. As the Manager points out, it is a good ploy for a wet summer afternoon.

After the death of Dr Joe Leckie, the whole weight of command devolved on Mr Gordon Leckie, and though Dr Strachan rendered a great deal of assistance until 1957 during his four-year period as Hydro doctor and assistant to Mr Gordon, the General Manager shouldered the complete responsibility for the day-to-day management in those years when the Establishment grew and prospered to limits which had not been thought possible. In May 1960, he fell ill and his younger son, Mr John Leckie, who at the time was managing the farms, was appointed Assistant Manager and Secretary.

On 1st August, William Gordon Leckie died at Strathearn Leigh, deeply mourned by a host of friends who included many of the regular visitors to the Hydro. He had been General Manager for only 12 years, but they were years of intense effort, mentally and physically, and, apart from the earliest decade of the Company, the most formative and crucial years in the history of the Hydropathic Establishment.

Just a matter of weeks later, the death occurred in Crieff of Major R. J. B. Sellar, a Director and enthusiastic member of the Company for 15 years.

To fill the vacancies existing on the Board it was agreed to ask Sir Malcolm Knox, Vice Chancellor and Principal of St. Andrews University—he had known the Hydro intimately for 30 years; Dr William Leckie, son of Dr Joe, and Mrs Marjory Leckie, widow of Mr Gordon, to accept office. This they did, the Board then being composed of Mr J. R. Donaldson (chairman), Mr J. A. Milligan, Mr G. L.

Barr, Mrs Barbara Leckie, Mr John Leckie, Sir Malcolm Knox, Mrs Marjory Leckie, and Dr William Leckie. Mr Milligan died in 1962, after ten years on the Board, and Mr Barr in 1964, after six years. Mr R. Graham Mickel, a solicitor in Crieff, was appointed a Director in 1965.

Reporting to the A.G.M. in 1960, the Chairman said it had been a very satisfactory year owing to more visitors over a longer period and better results from farm and laundry. The policy of the Directors continued to be to build up liquid reserves and to plough back large sums to maintain the buildings in good repair. That policy, it is good to know, still holds.

Developments in the course of the last seven years have kept pace with modern trends, the most important being the installation of two oil-fired boilers in place of the coal-burning monsters. The new system, which began operating in August 1966, is completely automatic and the boilers can be operated together as one unit or quite independently of one another. The burnt gases are carried off to the tall chimney in the wood. These boilers have meant a great saving in manpower and cost, as well as being so much cleaner than the old coal boilers.

Parts of the basement corridor, culminating at the west end of the building in the drying room, remind one of the bowels of a ship—pipes of half a dozen sizes stretching into the distance, wires, single and in bundles, inextricably mixed or mingled, and all sorts of clicks and clacks, whirrings and hissings heard, especially in the quiet times, add to the illusion.

Here and in the sub-basement are the workshops of joiner, plumber, upholsterer—the old Turkish bath is used by the painter while the cooling-off room is now the television room—together with the filtration plant for the swimming pool and inspection passages for plumbing and electrical systems.

At the east end of the basement—incidentally, owing to the slope of the ground, this floor level is open to the south—lie the kitchen premises. And how important these are is appreciated by all and not only by the housewives among the visitors. Gas and steam are used in cooking, the gas range being the main operating unit. The bakehouse or Scotch oven, 80 years old in 1965, was replaced by a modern, oil-fired one and in January 1966, the two bakers started making all the bread required, thus following the practice of pre-war days. Some figures of production are given in an appendix.

The price of food and the rates of wages were increasing each year, but the Hydro attracted more and more people each year; so much so that in 1962 it was decided that the undertaking of wedding receptions, dinners and dinner-dances would have to be stopped as "the House was so busy with resident guests that those functions were a burden to the staff and, considering the extra work and disruption of the routine, a poor financial return".

It was just as well this decision had been taken, for in January and February 1964, 3050 letters came asking for reservations for the summer months. A number of those, as well as many telephone enquiries, had to be refused—a measure of the amazing popularity of the Hydro.

Mention has been made from time to time of the growing numbers of children being brought to the House. In July 1966, the total of young people in the nursery rose to such a height that a bedroom had to be brought into use as a temporary dining room for them. The daily average of children in the House throughout the year is 25.

Of the outside interests of the Company the noteworthy features in recent years have been the new building at Dallerie Laundry which has enabled the whole business of Dallerie and Strathearn Laundries to be conducted in one centre since 1966, when the Strathearn Steam Laundry Company was taken over; the conversion of the electric supply from direct to alternating current, about which more is said in the chapter on electricity; the sale of Ardrostan farmhouse to the Merchant Company of Edinburgh as an outdoor centre for pupils; and of 15 acres of the ground there to Perthshire Caravan Company; the taking over of the Colony Farm, on the south side of the Perth road, for raising beef; and the formation of a forest nursery in a part of

Strathearn Leigh Garden, with 40,000 seedlings for replanting on the estate.

So the organisation and work of the Strathearn Hydropathic Establishment Company goes on, unceasing, requiring vigilance and care, but rewarding in the pleasure given to thousands, year in year out.

A DAY IN THE LIFE OF THE HYDRO

"Handsome is that handsome does."

GOLDSMITH

Twenty-four hours a day, seven days a week and for 52 weeks in the year the Hydro Management are responsible and caring for the welfare of their guests. You recall J. J. Bell's remark that "the wheels went round, and nothing ever seemed to interrupt their smooth and steady revolution". Any business man or capable housewife knows, without deep thought, that that sort of efficiency is achieved only by long planning and hard work on the part of everyone, from the Manager downwards.

For a few minutes let us watch the staff "drill" go into action on the arrival of one of the families we introduced to you at the start of our story. They are new to the Hydro, so, while Dad goes to sign the register and discover their room numbers, Mummy supervises the transfer of luggage from car to trolley.

"Where are our rooms," she asks the porter when Father comes back.

"They're up the Pulpit Stairs," he says, and receives a look of astonishment in return.

He might just as well have said, "They're in the 'Doctor's Attic'," for all it conveys to the newcomers.

The "Pulpit Stairs" are the short flights leading to bedrooms to the front or south side of the House, while the "Doctor's Attic" is towards the west end of the main building and contains four bedrooms, quite separate from the others.

The porter takes the trolley up in the luggage lift while the family follow in the passenger lift and duly arrive at their bedrooms. As they are settling in a knock is heard and when invited to "Come in" there enters a lady, quiet of manner and very much at home, who explains that she is the hostess and has come to welcome them to the Hydro and to hope that they will enjoy their stay. She assures herself that the accommodation is right; tells them to let her know if they require anything; where they will find the nursery for the smaller children; and that lunch will be on in quarter of an hour.

This gracious idea originated with Mrs Barbara Leckie when she became hostess in 1952 and has been carried on in the same way since she retired in 1965. In addition to welcoming the guests on arrival the hostess sees them and chats to them during afternoon tea, and in these ways helps them to feel that they are already of the "family". She speedily becomes known to everyone, for she is their direct link with the Management.

In a small hotel a gesture of this kind is easy, though that does not mean that it is always made, but in a place the size of Strathearn House with its 200 bedrooms and over 300 people in the busy season it is a most valuable policy to prevent an impersonal atmosphere from developing.

Other steps to counteract any trend of that nature include the tennis tournament always held on Mondays; the Wednesday golf competition and, of course, a number of dances on the programme each evening. All of these are pleasant "mixers" and help to overcome any shyness or reticence on the part of new arrivals. Very soon they are all, old and young, in the swim.

At seven o'clock each morning the building begins to come alive, for the Hydro 'bus arrives at that time with a number of housemaids who start to clean the public rooms and, where desired, to serve early morning tea. At eight o'clock the 'bus arrives again with some of the waitresses, whose final preparations for breakfast are made—morning rolls, butter, milk and marmalade to all tables.

Breakfast, beginning at 8.30 a.m., is one of the busiest meals of the day, and the stillroom where the waitresses pick up their orders, belies its name as at no other time. It is by no means still. Coffee or tea—perhaps both—and toast have to go to every table as well as whatever courses are required. Not many visitors ask for breakfast in bed—except on New Year's Day!

By the time breakfast has begun one member of the office staff is at work, the others arriving at nine o'clock, and the office is open then, without a break, until 10 p.m., the staff taking "staggered" meal times. The senior staff are Miss Stenhouse, Miss McLean, the cashier, and the head receptionist, Miss Norris. The first office duties are to bring guests' bills up-to-date and insert any extras which may have been noted by the dining room or elsewhere. The day's mail has to be answered and the menus duplicated, lists of departures and arrivals for the following day made out, and a copy given to the manageress of the dining room and heads of other departments. Details of numbers in each party arriving, how many children and whether they will take meals in the children's dining room or with their parents, are all given in the list, and the manageress then plans how best to fit them in.

She has in the dining room 16 "stations" for waitresses, and each girl attends six or seven tables in her "station". Once breakfast is over the vacuum cleaners come out and the dining room is cleaned and tables re-arranged for parties arriving before lunch time. Tables can be built up to take six or eight of one party, and though it is not often that more than eight ask to be seated together it can be done if required.

Early in the forenoon the Chef begins to order provisions and make up his menus for the following day—how much of this, how much of that? This is where years of experience tell; but even that quality can be upset—by the weather or by some unexpected trend of taste. If the morning starts off grey and miserable and cold, lots of soup will be wanted at lunch time, and hot main dishes. By midday, when all these are cooking, out comes the sun, dispersing the clouds, killing the wind and promising a really hot afternoon. Soup is out; fruit juice is in; salads and cold meats become the favourites, with ice cream to follow. Who would be a Chef?

Housemaids begin operations in their own section of bedrooms while breakfast is being served, and they work on until lunch time.

Many of the staff are off duty in the afternoon so that tea, between four and five o'clock, is served by waitresses who came up from the town specially to do this. Afternoon tea is quite a lively social occasion and a time for much chatter and laughter throughout the winter garden and ball room.

Two hours before dinner the kitchen staff are at work again and they ultimately finish their day's darg about 8 p.m. The waitresses, having cleared their tables of all signs of dinner, lay them for breakfast, and go off.

All through the day there have been two porters on duty, and this holds throughout the night as well, when special patrols have to be made. Twice during the night one or other of the men on duty makes a tour of the whole building. About two o'clock and again about four o'clock they go round, carrying with them a small clock which, when a special key is inserted in it and turned, stamps the time on a paper disc inside the clock. There are ten of these special keys, hung in particular parts of the House, and every point has to be visited on each round so that the exact time when that area of the building was visited can be registered. These rounds, are, of course, precautions against fire.

Somewhere between ten o'clock and midnight, dependent upon other calls, shoe cleaning is done, usually by hand, but if footwear is very dirty then the electric cleaning machine is used.

The Company's tradesmen—joiners, plumbers, painters, electrician, upholsterer—are on the job each day. Before they begin they consult a large note book in the Manager's office in which they find, written down by the house-keeper, the house manageress, the assistant manager or the Manager himself, notes on repairs or replacements to be immediately attended to. In fact, anyone on the staff who has seen or has been told of some defect is expected to note it in this book. In this way the upkeep of the huge building and all its equipment is looked after; door locks are repaired, vacuum cleaners are repaired, electric light bulbs replaced, choked drains are freed, carpets kept in good shape, and so on through all the many jobs of house maintenance. No wonder so many expressions of pleasure in the spruce, tidy and bright appearance of the House are passed by visitors.

The Management have no lack of problems. Securing and retaining staff tends to be a permanent headache, particularly acute in the spring when hotels that have been closed during the winter open up again and are looking for waitresses, housemaids, and kitchen staff.

Another grave difficulty can be the risk of infection—any infection—amongst the visitors, and there is always the likelihood of any illness whatever being blamed on the immediate surroundings and circumstances. The Hydro Management, therefore, take very great care in matters of hygiene in order to reduce the possibility of infection to a minimum. To this end also they have a very close link with the Professor of Public Health in the University of Dundee.

The Manager sees the heads of departments at some time or other every day, and with a "personal paging system" somewhat reminiscent of "The Man From U.N.C.L.E." he can be in touch with them very quickly. There are seven of these electronic receivers, and by means of them the office can contact the persons carrying them. They are used mainly by the porters and the housekeeping staff.

Here again is evidence of up-to-the-minute thinking and modern practice, two qualities in which the Company has never, over the past 100 years, been lacking.

FUN AND GAMES

"Life's a pleasant institution
Let us take it as it comes."

GILBERT

Dr Meikle forgot nothing.

Well he knew that scores of people could not live together without some mutual interest or entertainment. In the first winter—1868–69—he had organised a "Conversazione" which was "favourably reported on" and approved by the Directors, who told him to arrange another at his discretion.

That is the first hint of recreation and diversion for the visitors, but it was followed speedily by other plans, for in October 1870, work was begun, as already mentioned, on recreation room (now the ballroom), gymnasium, billiard room and bowling alley. A bowling green also proved an attraction in the early years but it vanished later, and when the matter of a new green was considered in 1931 it was decided not to proceed in view of facilities offered by the Crieff club. *Mens sana in corpore sano.* To-day the Hydro offers facilities for many amusements and recreations— table tennis, badminton, billiards, swimming, tennis, golf, croquet, putting, riding and water ski-ing.

The gymnasium probably did exist, though there is none now. The recreation hall, completed and opened in June 1871, afforded, state the minutes, "much relief in the arrangements and service of the House, and great satisfaction and enjoyment to the visitors, all who had been in the House before the Hall was erected expressing almost astonishment at the improvement. The American Bowling Alley is also in full working order, and seems to be much appreciated". Where the alley was and when it 'folded up' are not recorded.

The visitors were not slow to make their own amusements, organising lectures, concerts and, in later years, other events when the official programme gave them a "breather".

A letter written by a visitor in May 1898, states that—"The house is very comfortable inside with a very agreeable company of from 150 to 200 visitors, all very nice people. Somehow they always manage to get up a very creditable concert after dinner in the drawing room, so that the time passes not so bad at all."

Sledging down the main drive became very popular in winter, in those days before the motor car monopolised the roads, and one of the really spectacular sights must have been to watch some of the livelier young men, immaculate in white ties and "tails", swinging over the swimming pool on the rings suspended from the roof.

To-day there are no rings. But redecoration and the installation of a filter plant have greatly increased the attraction of the pool. Many will remember that before that plant was installed the water had a gloomy appearance. This was attributed to the peat in the water and the swimming pool attendant would make a dubious show of its clarity by filling a tumbler from the pool and holding it up to the light. On one occasion, the attendant, who was a keen fisherman, was given a fish by a friendly guest and this he had left uncovered on a shelf in the swimming pool. A lady brought her young child down for a swim and nothing could convince her that the fish had not been removed from the pool. The swimming lesson was abandoned forthwith.

Nowadays races to the top of the Knock, in daylight and in dark, but preferably, perhaps, in moonlight, keep the younger element amused. Water ski-ing is now a strong attraction and can be practised on all suitable afternoons in the summer from the Hydro's own stretch of beach on Loch Earn. Rowing and sailing, the latter with the Loch Earn Sailing School, can also be found at St. Fillans.

Tennis, one of the three oldest games mentioned in the Company's records, retains its great popularity. Tournaments take place once a week in the high season—one for juniors only, and one for all. There are two red blaes courts and three all-weather, and they are much used. The game is mentioned in minutes of the Board more than 90 years ago. A note from a meeting on 20th December, 1876 reads:

Lawn Tennis—As this game, which had been much asked for last summer, was injurious to the croquet and bowling greens, it was agreed that part of the ground to the north of the House, formerly thought of for a new bowling green, should be prepared for this.

Tennis on the bowling green! How the keen bowlers must have loved that!

The proposed position for the new courts would be exactly where they are now.

Other developments in the facilities for this game occurred from time to time. For example, in 1885, the Directors decided to make "another cinder or sand court to the east of the dining room", and the following year they agreed to form "a concrete tennis court 60 yards by 15 yards which could be flooded in winter for skating and curling". Whether these suggestions came to anything is not stated, no further word of tennis appearing again for many years. Certainly no mention is made of curling or skating in the winters following. Listed amongst the improvements made during 1916–17 are "red ash tennis courts", and at the end of 1923 it was arranged to lay down two En-Tout-Cas courts in place of the old grass courts, and this was done.

For a number of years now a special week-long competition is held each summer, when prizes for all classes of play are presented at a ball on the Friday evening.

Golf, of course, has for long been one of the major games indulged in by the Hydropathic visitors, and the Directors did much to encourage this. The first Crieff golf course named in the records is Ledbowie Park, which lies more than a mile from the town on the south side of the Comrie road and opposite the Granite Lodge—the first lodge of Ochtertyre House as one travels west. That meant a long tramp for players before and after a game, but it was used to some extent by guests at the Hydro, for in April 1892, Mr Lewis Miller, a timber merchant and prominent Crieff citizen, wrote to the Directors asking for a contribution of £25 towards Crieff Golf Club, of which he was president. They sent him £20 "on condition that the visitors in the Establishment have the liberty of using the course at Ledbowie Park".

Within a year the club had moved to fields at Culcrieff, on the north side of the Knock and only about ten minutes walk from the House, a fact which made the Directors contribute £35 to the club, "largely taken advantage of by the visitors, on condition that the visitors at the Hydro have the free use of the course for one year".

Other developments followed until, in 1896, an arrangement was reached with the club that the Hydro's annual payment should be increased from £35 to £57 10s., the Company to have equal rights with the club to the use of the greens, and to be at liberty to erect a golf house for their own visitors. This happy state of affairs lasted only until 1905 when an intimation received from Crieff Golf Club stated "that owing to the number of players (especially poor players) the arrangement made with the Club some years ago, for Hydro visitors being free, will terminate next May."

From that point nothing more is recorded of the golf club until after the Company entered into possession of Ferntower House and lands, when the new constitution had as its first resolution the laying out of a golf course and recreation ground. That was in May 1913, and by October of the same year Crieff Golf Club proposed to feu the lower fields of Ferntower—about 100 acres—and put up a club-house to the west of the Callum's Hill entrance gate. The difference in the new contract between the Company and the club was that Hydro guests were to use the course on the same terms as other visitors; also, that ground for a club-house would be feued to the club. This was done and the rent fixed at £120 per annum. Ten years later (1924) a 19-years lease at £150 rent for the first five years and £180 for the remainder was offered, and with a view to carrying out improvements the club were to get a report from James Braid, then one of the greatest experts in this work.

A feature of the summer schedule at the Hydro has, for many years, been the weekly golf tournament, run on Stableford lines, which gives much enjoyment and not a little amusement.

One other highly popular recreation enjoyed by young

and old alike, is dancing. In the high season, four nights each week the ballroom comes alive with whirling lights and bright reflections from mirrors and from ladies' evening wear ornaments and jewellery, while the pulse stirs to the beat of the band, throbbing through hall and winter garden.

It is thrilling to see the ballroom ablaze with full lighting and crammed with Scottish country dance sets doing "The Duke of Perth". The spectators beat time and they applaud just as enthusiastically as the dancers when the music stops. Mothers with small sons, fathers with tiny daughters who look like fairies, dance "The Dashing White Sergeant". To enjoy all this is to savour one attractive aspect of life at the Hydro which appeals to everyone's spirit of youth and fun and happy leisure.

In contrast, to see the whole area of the ballroom and the winter garden in its still cheerful but quieter afternoon atmosphere of chattering tea tables; or, in early afternoon on sunny days, to find it silent and drowsy, is but to experience further, attractive facets of this "stately pleasure dome".

The Chairman brought before the meeting the proposal of Mr John Welsh Leith, to provide a band of Musicians for some of the summer months.

That minute of April 1902, is the first suggestion of a "band of Musicians" at the Hydro, and alas! there is no further mention of them, so we do not know whether or not they were engaged.

For a time, after a band was employed, the pianist filled the double role of band leader and organist at the evening service. At a fixed time each evening dancing stopped. The lights in the ballroom and winter garden were lowered, and a few minutes later the service in the drawing room began. There is a story that the pianist, a Mr Turner, caught unexpectedly by the lowering of the lights, sped through to the organ, and absent-mindedly opened the service with a few, brisk bars of the polka he had just stopped playing on the piano.

The highlight of a girl's holiday came if she happened to be dancing "the prayer dance", as the dance before the service came to be called, with the boy of her choice. Together they walked into the drawing room; they sat together, and they shared a hymnbook!

Tuesday and Thursday evenings are "bandless", but the former sees the hostess entertaining the enthusiasts and tyros by teaching country dancing, an instruction class that has been responsible for introducing a great army of regular visitors from all parts of Great Britain and overseas to those invigorating and companionable dances.

Thursday evenings are given over to young people to join in some communal ploy or to use their ingenuity to find amusements for themselves and others. Treasure hunts, using dad's or mum's car, were popular for many years until the traffic on the roads became too intense for these to be run safely. Sausage "sizzles" in the woods around the Knock also found favour, while other sources of fun were barn dances, complete with competitions for neatest ankles or knobbliest knees.

Table tennis tournaments, for various age groups, putting competitions for everyone, and, in far-off days, bowling and croquet tournaments—all have given fun and pleasure.

The playing of cards, like alcoholic beverages, was banned in the early years, but military whist has for long been enjoyed by many and still goes on, though whist itself has given way to bridge. Private bridge fours are readily established amongst the residents and holiday visitors. For those who do not play there is the solace of books or the excitement of the television room. New books are bought twice a year for the Hydro library.

The Christmas and New Year weeks are not quite like any other times. Parties, small and large, go on at all spare moments—before lunch, before dinner, during the dance programme interval, and possibly even later. Walks are nearly always possible on some of the days, and the Knock is a favourite stroll. Throughout the day the children have their Christmas gifts and games to amuse them, and in the evening, as well as dancing a good deal of bridge is played.

Walking, of course, has always been the simplest form of

exercise and here, once again, the Hydro scores. Whether for a quiet saunter around the grounds or the paths of the Knock; the rather longer walk through the MacRosty Park or by Lady Mary's Walk along the north bank of the River Earn; or a real day's hill walking on Perthshire's Ben Vorlich, Schiehallion, Ben Lawers, Ben Chonzie and many others, Strathearn House is an ideal centre.

The Knock, of course, has its own stories. It was the scene, in 1563, of the burning of Kate Macnevin, a reputed witch, on a bluff on the north side still known as "Kate Macnevin's Craig". It possesses a huge "cradle-stone" or rocking stone which, the story goes, was once split by lightning. And near the stone was a well—the Kinkhoast Well; kinkhoast being the old Scots word for whooping-cough. Parents took their children to drink the water and breathe the fine, caller air, in the belief that that would cure them.

Since about 1950, when Dr Joe and Mrs Barbara Leckie moved from Edinburgh to the Hydro permanently, and she transferred her riding stable from the city to the Establishment stables, facilities for riding and learning to ride have been available. When Mrs Leckie retired from active participation in the running of the Hydro, at the end of 1965, the Company took over the 14 ponies.

It is a pleasing picture, on summer mornings, to see very small children being given first lessons in horsemanship, and to watch their confidence growing day by day.

This topic may bring back happy memories to those who were small children in the 'Fifties and who rode on the back of Angelina, the donkey, whose bray could be heard all over the grounds and which, at first acquaintance, caused great alarm amongst the "small fry".

By a judicious mixing of some of the above-mentioned pastimes—not forgetting the physical value of relaxation or just plain laziness—the holiday hours and weeks at the Hydro slip past all too quickly.

HYDRO ELECTRICITY

"Early Electric! With what radiant hope
Men formed this many-branched electrolier . . ."
BETJEMAN

Those who frequent the Hydro at almost any season of the year, but particularly in August, September and at Christmas, know well the large proportion of visitors from the North-east shires of England. Northumberland and Durham, with the towns of Newcastle and Sunderland, have for many years staunchly supported Crieff Hydropathic, many visitors coming twice a year, so that their cars know every mile of the road and could almost make it without human interference.

Quite apart from the fact that the whole family enjoys the amenities of the Establishment—perhaps the men most of all, for they feel they are getting value for money—how many of them, I wonder, ever give a thought to the earliest "explorers" from their countryside, of Crieff and its Hydro? It is not easy to discover the source from which this popularity of Strathearn House grew, but it could well go back 80 years.

We know that the Company's first minute book ends in May 1889, with a decision to instal electric light into the public rooms. In December of the previous year there appears a minute which says:

"Estimate by a Newcastle firm for lighting the public rooms by electricity at a cost of £600. Further inquiries before doing this."

Two months before this Dr Meikle had been instructed to make enquiry as to the cost of using electricity in the public rooms, "especially with the view of making these rooms more easily ventilated". Twelve years before, the drawing room had been enlarged and decorated, so it was judged time for re-doing it; and like prudent housewives planning their work, the Directors decided to instal electric light before redecorating.

One presumes that the Newcastle firm, Messrs Holmes, visited the Hydro before submitting an estimate and saw for themselves the kind of place it was.

That is the first link with the North-east of England, but 12 years later another tie was formed. The firm of Richardson and Co., Darlington, in 1902, sent in a design for a Winter Garden, which the Board were considering as an addition to the front of the building. We know that Richardson's tender was accepted. Those two contacts constitute the first mention of North-east England interest in the Hydro. Who is to say that one or other of those business visits did not spark off a move among the shrewd people of that area towards the not-too-distant holiday town of Crieff?

Whatever the result in that direction, the electricity project went ahead.

Reference is made in a later chapter to one, James Rigg, a plumber, who became almost the best-informed man on the electrical plant details. Though he *may* not have been on the staff of the Hydro when the first generator was installed, he made himself acquainted with all the details and put them on paper—small scraps of paper which he signed but usually did not date. One or two have 1917 on them, so it looks as if he had been asked to write out this information. He says:

"1889. The Electric Light was first installed; The Dynamo was Driven by Gas Engine. Engine by Dick, Kerr and Coy, Kilmarnock. 52 Accumulators, and wiring installed by Anderson and Monro, Glasgow. Makers of Dynamo, 'Pairs and Scott'. Mr Yeaman was Consulting Engineer. The Accumulators were charged during day time. Lighting off the accumulators during night time at 100 Volts; Only in the Dining Room, Drawing Room, Ladies' writing Room, Recreation Hall, Office, and Main Corridor was the Electric Light Installed; A 16 candle power Ediswan Lamp cost 5s each then. The Accumulators cost £300; these were renewed once."

"1899 Decr. 19th. Current first switched on to Hydro; Messrs. Lowdon installed a Parker Dynamo at Powerhouse and a Parker Balancer at Hydro. A 12″ Steel pipe laid from Powerhouse to Croy, by our own workmen."

But more of that later development in a moment.

Inside the House the cables leading to the actual lights were not built into the walls or panelling; not even boxed in in any way at first. They just hung loose along the walls or across the ceilings. "Much too dangerous with this new thing to close 'em in. Might set fire to the house any minute." So wires festooned the walls and ceiling even of the beautifully re-decorated drawing room which was very much admired.

The switch-on of the new system took place probably in the spring of 1890, and for nearly ten years the plant operated without too many or too infuriating breakdowns.

Having electricity in the House meant other things besides light. It was agreed in 1896 to procure electric fans for ventilation and a refrigerator for the meat larder. Shortly after that came the astonishing news that in Fort Augustus and Fort William they were generating electricity from waterfalls in those districts, and someone on the Board said, "What about it? We could do that."

The matter was brought up at the next meeting, on 5th May 1897.

"There is a proposal to utilise the Falls of Barvick as a source of power for electric lighting. The Directors will try to ascertain how far this may be turned to account for the benefit of the Company and will be guided accordingly."

It does not, unfortunately, tell us who first put forward the suggestion, but less than a year later comes a note that some delay had been caused to the improvements on the ladies' bathroom "by the extent of the excavations under the bathroom to obtain space for additional Electric Storage Batteries and the catacomblike passage giving access to the supply and waste pipes".

Once more Sir Patrick Keith Murray showed his good-will. Dr Meikle told the Board that Mr David Keith Murray had called on him on 5th August (1898), and intimated that Sir Patrick was willing that the Company should have an opportunity of considering the suitability of the Barvick as a source of power for Electric Lighting. Dr Thomas went on to give a detailed account of what had since been done in the matter and read correspondence anent water pipes, turbines, dynamos, etc.; also a letter stating that Sir Patrick would give the land (not exceeding five acres) for the Reservoir at 50s. per acre per annum feu duty; wayleave for the pipes and wires etc. ($2\frac{1}{2}$ miles) for 10s. per annum, and land for cottages, turbines and dynamos (not exceeding one acre) at £10 per acre. The Board decided to go ahead and obtain estimates.

Meetings with a Mr Lowden, an electrical engineer from Dundee, and with a Mr Powell, a civil engineer from London, were reported in December 1898. Lowden suggested limiting the scheme for the present, by omitting the reservoir and taking the water supply from a lower level, giving a head of water of about 500 feet. The cost was to be about £3,000.

Using the Barvick for power meant that the whole Hydro was to be lit by electricity, and at the annual general meeting in '99 the report stated that some progress had been made and it seemed likely that the scheme would be completed in two or three months. This did not quite come off, for there were delays in the delivery of the dynamo and the pipes, but the current came through for the first time on 19th December 1899, "giving much satisfaction to the visitors, and giving the whole Establishment a bright look".

What a day that must have been! Outside the cities and some large towns there was literally nothing like it in any private building, except the Benedictine monastery at Fort Augustus.

Mention was made a page or so back of Fort Augustus and Fort William, the reason being that they were the first two places in Scotland to be lit by electricity generated by water power. In a paper written a few years ago, Mr R. B. Anderson, chairman of the Scottish Branch of the Institution of Electrical Engineers, said:

"All the essential technical inventions and discoveries had certainly been made many years before 1890. Nevertheless, it seems quite remarkable to me that the monks of St. Benedict's Abbey, in remote Fort Augustus, were so well informed that within eight years of the first experimental station being established in London they were able to bring into operation their own plant and distribution system."

These words might almost have been written about the Directors of Crieff Hydropathic, they too, were pioneering this wonderful new system of lighting, long before it became the universal service it now is. The Abbey had their hydrogenerator going in 1890 and, I believe, ultimately supplied the village. Their neighbour, Fort William, followed suit in 1896, and Crieff Hydro in 1899—the first three stations of this kind in Scotland.

A year or two passed before it became obvious that a dam built on the Barvick would give a steadier flow of water to the generator, but snags appeared because the same water had also to drive the mill-wheels of several mill-owners farther down stream. It was not until 1907 that the Board cleared this hurdle and by the end of November of that year the work was completed, thanks largely to the indefatigable James Lamb, who had been taken on as a bathman and joiner in 1871, and who was at the time of his death in 1912, Master of Works. I shall have more to say about this remarkable man elsewhere.

The civil engineer in charge, Mr Cowan, Glasgow, expressed himself as pleased with the finished job, and it is noted that the reservoir had greater capacity than expected. In 1910 repairs were done to some leaks in the embankment of the dam, but on 24th August, "in consequence of what seemed a Cloud-burst on the hills above the Barvick. . . . the Overflow of the Dam was much damaged, the flow of water over the weir (which is 42 feet wide) was 4½ feet deep. The lower half of the weir was carried away making a gap 21 feet deep. It required 16 tons of cement and the work of 10 men for 6 or 7 weeks to repair the damage done." The menace of this day can be realised when it is stated that two and a half inches of rain fell in the 24 hours. The rainfall for that month totalled 11½ inches, an extraordinary amount for any month of the year at Crieff.

From about this time the electricity supply becomes an

accepted amenity, giving little trouble and ever-widening service.   Indeed, even before it became infallible Dr Meikle announced that he wanted to use it for medical purposes. That was April, 1902, and that same year the Directors approved the use of an electric motor to help with the work in bakehouse and kitchen, while the thrashing mill was worked by electric current and the stables and coach-house were lit by it.

We in this seventh decade of the twentieth century imagine that we are slap-up-to-date with our dish-washing machine, our "frig", etc.   The Hydro, in 1904, had an electric knife cleaner on trial.   (There were no such things as stainless steel knives and forks in those days.)   An electric dish washer was on order, and a few years later a vacuum cleaner costing £270 was bought.   The Directors were very much "with it".

One matter which had to be accepted for a long time was the short black-out, twice a day.   These occurred soon after 8 a.m. and 5 p.m., and were caused by a necessary change-over from one generator to another.   Occasions did arise when the current failed for some other reason, and on one of these there hangs a tale.   Chatting with the head porter, then Andrew Cairns, one of the guests asked if power cuts often occurred.

"Oh, no," replied Cairns.   "But there was one a few months back that lasted a whilie.   I had to go round wi' candles.   An' ye know, sir, there wasny a bedroom in the Hydro that didny have a bottle to put a candle in."

There had been an electric bell system throughout the House from the earliest days, but six years after the opening it is reported as being very defective.   Dr Meikle, therefore, spoke to a Mr Gilbert, electrician to the North British Railway Company, who was staying in the Hydro, and he undertook to put the system into an efficient state for £120, and the board and lodging of his men.

By 1886 the bell wires had "lost their guttapercha coating and were not working properly", and in making the repairs the following year three and a half miles of new wire had to be used. This time the wiring lasted longer for it was not till 1912 that replacements had to be carried out.

James Caw, who had been house steward before having to leave through illness and who returned as cashier some years later, tells in a little book he wrote that he had a "bee in his bonnet" about the bell system, and thought about it night and day, seven days a week. He even found himself drawing pencil lines "as electric wires, in the kirk on my clean wristbands". He goes on:

"There were fully three miles of wires here, there, and every-where, some of them bare, and bells ringing continually . . . Ultimately, a splendid system was organised, whereby a first push shows the number in the case and rings; then a connecting wire calls down the maid, if in her attic-bedroom at the time. A second ring (showing 'neglect') is immediately signalled in the office. I also wished that of the various indicators—six on each floor—the bells were not to sound during the night, for fear of disturbing the sleepers—but only to indicate the numbers. This puzzled the expert a bit at first; but I took him to where I had it working in the new wing—my own invention. There is an electric indicating case in the shoe hall, from which the night porter knows which floor to go to, and an electric observation case on each landing to guide him to the case where the number is shown. The installation cost £225. Eighteen domestic telephones throughout the house cost £112. There are nine telephone instruments in the office; and oh, what a Babel at times! Electricity for everything! There is an electric hoist, an electric vacuum cleaner, an electric shoe brushing-machine, and electric dish washing-machine, an electric knife-cleaner, an electric bread-toaster, an electric-driven grindstone. There are three 'phone cabinets, with three junction lines to Crieff Ex-change; also four internal stations, one of which goes to the kitchen for 'phoning direct from that department to Edinburgh, Glasgow, Perth, or anywhere for food supplies. The 'phone calls used each year number 14,000; the total sum reaching to £60 annually; likewise, £145 for the payment of 'trunk' fees. Altogether the Establishment is a most wonderful piece of 'clockwork'."

Finally, a word about modern times. As many of the men living in the House have found to their dismay, only direct current flowed through the cables. Most electric razors take both types of current, and if one was cunning and knew where to look in the bedrooms—the underside of the wall light switch—one found there a two-pin socket to take the shaver's plug. If the razor could not digest D.C. then a walk to the gentlemen's wash-room on the ground floor was necessary, for there there is a wall socket giving alternating current. This comes from the national grid, to which the whole of the ground floor was converted in 1962.

At the moment of writing this chapter plans are in hand for converting the whole system to A.C. It is expected that in the centenary year the Hydropathic will be ready to take all its electric supply from the national grid system. This change has been dictated by the Loch Turret Water Board's decision to divert the flow from the Barvick Falls— thereby from the Company's Pelton wheel at a little station in the Turret valley—to the town of Grangemouth. By this move, the right of the Hydropathic Company since 1898 to the use of this water has been taken away, and the more-or-less silent protests of gentlemen who have had to shave in the wash-room have been answered.

Sandy Mitchell, who succeeded James Rigg as electrician, supplies the note on which to round off this chapter. Sandy was a fanatic in his love of his pipes and wires—also in his dislike of painters who seemed to enjoy covering up his work. His invariable reply to Dr Leckie or Mr Gordon Leckie, if they told him to change something—the position of a light or a switch in a bedroom—was, simply, "Ay, ay!" Into that exclamation he could put a world of feeling, and on one occasion, when the Doctor, exasperated by those mono-syllables, asked what he meant by "Ay, ay!" Sandy replied,

"I hear what ye say, but I dinna think much o'it."

"WATER IS BEST"

"...... 'Tis a little thing
To give a cup of water."

TALFOURD

Ἄριστον μὲν ὕδωρ, "Water is best". That is the motto of Crieff Hydropathic, and though the sense of these three words, taken out of context, is not what the Greek poet Pindar intended, for he was writing of the translucence of liquids, there is no doubt that, when they were chosen, a hundred years ago, it was to represent the strong belief of a very large number of people in the "water cure".

Hydropathy is, or perhaps more correctly, *was* the art of treating diseases by the application of water in various ways and at differing temperatures. Water was used from ancient times in both acute and chronic diseases, particularly in fevers, but it was a Silesian farmer, Vincent Priessnitz, who developed the "science of hydropathy", using water alone to cure disease. He also recommended a rather ascetic way of life, alcohol, tea and coffee being forbidden and pure air and exercise being very much encouraged. Used with his insight and commonsense, and largely employing the physical properties of water without claiming any real pharmacological action, Priessnitz was very successful. However, many of those who followed him claimed almost magical powers for their brand of the science, and this brought hydropathy into disrepute in certain quarters.

The advance of therapeutics has been so great in the past 30 years and drugs are now so potent, that it is difficult for us to recognise that hydropathy in the 1850's was good treatment, particularly when compared with most other medical treatment then in vogue. At the worst it was harmless, while the others tended to be either variations on the theme of catharsis (violent purgative measures) or blood-letting, both, in fact, usually doing more harm than good.

At any rate, towards the middle of the nineteenth century hydropathics sprang up like mushrooms all over the United Kingdom, often purporting to be sited strategically over life-giving springs of water.

The first hydro in Scotland was the Glenburn, situated a little way up the hillside and looking north-west across Rothesay Bay to that magnificent scene of hills and sea-lochs which border the waters of the bay like multi-coloured gems in a giant necklace.

It was opened in 1843 by Dr William Paterson who had studied under Priessnitz, and consisted of a mansion house bought but not built for the purpose. The present structure was completed in 1894 after a fire in 1891 which destroyed the original and its additions which accommodated in all about 200 visitors. Three years later Dr Rowland East opened a small hydro at Kirn Pier, near Dunoon, and it was here that Dr John Stuart Blackie, Professor of Humanity at Aberdeen, wrote a series of five letters on the water cure. These were first published in the *Aberdeen Herald* and then issued as a pamphlet.

In the meantime the Glasgow Hydropathic Society was formed for the purpose of broadcasting information about hydropathy by means of the Press, lectures and talks, social meetings, and whatever other means could be devised, and it was through the efforts of this society that Dr Alexander Munro became interested in the subject. Here the neophyte is not a qualified medical man but a minister in a small country church at Skene, in Aberdeenshire.

His health giving him concern, he studied hydropathy and ultimately, with the full agreement of his little church, began the study of medicine at Aberdeen University. After leaving the University he opened, in 1850, a small hydropathic at Angusfield, near Aberdeen. To mark this event a number of his friends and patients gave him a dinner at which Professor Blackie presided.

Angusfield, however, was vacated the following year in favour of Loch-Head mansion and grounds, Aberdeen, and this new property he converted into a hydropathic establishment and sanatorium. All through this period of studying and

PLATE 5

The Children's Paddling Pool

The Children's Playground

PLATE 6

The Bowling Green

The Riding School

of carrying on these hydros Dr Munro was still minister of the church at Skene, and he continued to be so for some time, driving over to Skene in his horse-drawn vehicle each Sunday accompanied by his family and perhaps a patient or two.

He had always taken a keen interest in writing about the water cure and as well as editing the *Aberdeen Water Cure Journal* he produced the *Family Hydropathic Guide* and other manuals of health.

William Meikle, who joined Munro in 1857 and took over Loch-Head when Munro went to Cluny Hills Hydropathic, Forres, must have been investigating hydropathy in his student days, for the thesis which gained him his degree of Doctor of Medicine was entitled "On some of the Actions and Uses of Water as a Therapeutic Agent". It may well be that his convictions on this subject swayed young Thomas towards the same way of thinking.

Whether or not that be so, Loch-Head went on in its smooth groove and everything seemed set for William Meikle to widen his knowledge and experience of hydropathy, with Thomas perhaps joining him when he graduated in 1861. He, William, had married about 1856 or 1857, but only 18 months after taking over Loch-Head he died. What happened in the interregnum between William's demise and Thomas buying Loch-Head from his brother's trustees is a matter for conjecture, but it seems likely, since Thomas clearly was interested in hydropathy, that he had supervised the running of the establishment, young though he was. Almost two years passed before Thomas came into possession and that may have been just as well, for he did not graduate until 1861.

When Dr Munro opened Loch-Head the equipment was somewhat primitive. Douches were given in a small wooden shed near the house; but the water for these had to be pumped from a stream nearby to a tank on the roof; and this was often done by the patients who were fit to do so. Gradually changes were made and appliances brought more up-to-date.

Dr Thomas Meikle took over complete control after graduation and worked hard and planned—and dreamed, too.

For before 1866 he had made up his mind to move nearer to the centre of Scottish affairs and of Scotland itself. He had seen and read of some of the large English hydropathic establishments; he knew the benefits of the Scottish air and the beauties of Scottish scenery; he must have known, also, the shrewdness of Scottish business men and his own powers of persuasion for a cause in which he implicitly believed.

He had, therefore, every right to dream—a dream that became Crieff Hydropathic Establishment—but of one thing we may be certain: that Thomas Meikle never dreamt that a day *might* come when alcoholic beverages might be sold in Strathearn House. And that day has not yet come. The Hydro has never held a liquor licence of any kind. This fact astonishes newcomers who, in the climate of present day opinion, find it hard to believe that so large and up-to-date an establishment can possibly pay its way without a licence.

Once upon a time a licence was applied for and was refused, and the whole business was so unusual that some account of it must be given. The time is October 1949.

A temperance establishment since its founding in 1868, the general feeling seemed to be against granting it even the "table licence" applied for, but the rejection of the application by the Central District Licensing Court of the County of Perth caused great dismay to Mr Gordon Leckie, the Manager, as he felt that the change in the habits of younger people, brought about by war-time experiences and life in the Armed Forces, would seriously militate against holidays in a "dry" hotel.

This belief, fortunately for the Hydro, turned out to be a mistaken one, as increasing arrivals in the years following the re-opening showed.

In the course of the hearing, which took place in the Town Hall in Crieff, the Chief Constable for the County, Mr A. Sim, said the premises were in excellent condition, but the applicant, Mr Gordon Leckie, while having business experience, had no knowledge of conducting licensed premises. A qualified assistant should be appointed. Mr

Sim had no objection to a licence provided it was of six-day duration and that no public bar was allowed. Mr Leckie agreed to meet those recommendations.

The objectors were the Rev. William Yule, South Church; the Rev. John Ferrie, North Church; and the Rev. John B. F. Montgomery, West Church, all of Crieff. They said that the granting of a licence to the Hydropathic would be a serious break in tradition which would be keenly felt by many who frequented the Hydro, so that they would cease to come.

The objectors believed, also, that the granting of a licence would be contrary to the known principles of the donors of certain Trusts. The founders of the Meikle Fund and the Paton Fund both held very strongly the same ideals of temperance as the founder of the Hydro, Dr Thomas Meikle, and these two Trusts would not have existed had the Hydropathic been a licensed house. The objectors believed, too, that any licence granted would adversely affect the amenity of the Hydro.

When Mr J. D. S. Miller, solicitor, Crieff, spoke of the character of the applicant, the objectors pointed out that they had nothing but respect for the personal integrity of the Manager and the greatest admiration for the way in which he had overcome many obstacles in getting the business into the splendid condition it was in. In Crieff they were proud of the Hydro and many would be sorry if a change in policy meant that the type of visitors who had frequented the town in the past would give way to another type altogether.

Mr Miller stated that the Trustees of these Funds were empowered, if they thought the Hydro not satisfactory, to provide benefits for ministers and their wives at some other establishment. Many people who had booked rooms, he said, had cancelled them on learning that there was no licence, while others had cut short their stay for the same reason. To hold no licence was a great disadvantage to the business. They wanted to encourage congresses and association meetings to come to Crieff but if refreshments could not be provided these would go elsewhere.

By a majority the Court refused the application.

The report in the local paper concluded: "This was the smallest attendance of Court members for a number of years, while the public attendance raised a new record for post-war years."

This application brought the word "liquor" into the Company's minutes for the first time since the Hydro opened, 81 years before. But it was not the first time that liquor had been spoken about—indeed, not the first time that liquor had appeared in the Hydro, tucked handily away at the bottom of the wardrobe.

When the practice of visitors taking their own supplies of liquor to the Hydro first began is not known, but, as any thinking individual could have forecast, there are almost as many stories concerned with drink as there are on all other topics put together, a not really surprising obsession in view of the strict regime within the House. That strict regime, even when allied to the sobriety, the firm discipline and the strong temperance beliefs of the great majority of guests in the House, did not blind Dr Meikle to what went on. And it should be said here and now that any drinking that went on in private was of the most harmless kind. Nobody got drunk: nobody was noisy. That was carefully seen to by Dr Meikle and his son, Dr Gordon Meikle, whose elder daughter, Mrs Honor Modjesky, writes to me from the U.S.A., as follows:

"Christmas at the Hydro was a very special time for me. On Christmas night the Meikles and the Duncans dined at the Hydro . . . There was a long table down the middle of the dining-room which was always decorated by a beautiful and original centrepiece. The bell would be rung and my father would say Grace and then we would tuck into a dinner, the size of which gives me indigestion to remember. Of course we danced it off! The after-dancing Hogmanay parties were legendary; my father and Uncle George (Duncan) spent most of the night patrolling the corridors to make sure the fun didn't get out of hand, and the empties retrieved from the wardrobe-tops would have stocked a distillery."

I know something about these Christmas and New Year

parties, and they are such pleasant and harmless social affairs that, in about 99 per cent. of cases the biggest kick the participants get is in the fact that they are doing this in an unlicensed hotel, with a most congenial crowd of people as their companions.

As Mrs Modjesky says, "My father and his brother-in-law, George Duncan, carried out my Grandfather's policies in their administration, while being a good deal more broadminded with regard to smoking and drinking."

One custom, introduced by Dr Meikle a very long time ago, was the glass of hot water, served to everyone in the entrance hall just before bedtime. This, of course, is an ancient medicament and, apart from the motto inscribed on the crockery and inlaid in the floor of the vestibule, was the last offering to Grecian origins of the water cure and "Water is Best". Attached to this custom are, naturally, stories of elderly gentlemen retiring to their bedrooms to lace the spring water with that other Highland "uisge beatha"—water of life—more commonly called whisky. Also of that naughty young fellow who poured a bottle or two of gin into the hot water and watched elderly ladies remarking on the purity of the water and asking for more.

I have remarked that virtually nothing escaped Dr Meikle, and any suggestion that he was in ignorance of the hot toddy practice—if, indeed, it was a practice—is belied by the story that, about 11 o'clock one evening, he met the night porter carrying a glass of steaming hot water along to a bedroom.

"Well, John, where are you taking that?"

"It's for 156, sir."

"What does he want hot water for at this time of night?"

"I think, maybe, it's for shavin', sir. He's likely going off wi' the early train." The porter is just covering up.

"In that case," says Dr Meikle, putting two fingers into a vest pocket and slipping something into the tumbler, "it'll be none the worse of a little bit of soap. It'll help it to lather."

For many years there stood in the hall a fountain, the water constantly running. First it was an erection of iron with drinking cup attached to it by a chain, and I have been assured that it was similar to those aged anachronisms that are still occasionally seen in village streets. Latterly, a marble-fronted fountain was put in and disappeared only about 20 years ago. One old lady asked me innocently if I knew the motto of the Hydro, and when I quoted "Water is best", she looked at me slyly and said "Yes. Water is best— taken in the right spirit," and waited to see if the *double entendre* registered.

The despondency felt as a result of the Licencing Court's decision in 1949 soon changed to relief.

The Directors were quick to realise that the fact that the hotel did not have a licence was one of the main reasons which made it such a desirable place for parents with young families to spend their holidays.

BENEFACTIONS TO THE CHURCH

"... and her name is Mrs Doasyouwouldbedoneby."
KINGSLEY

Several aspects of the Hydro Establishment keep cropping up in conversation whenever two or three persons who are staying or have stayed there meet, and almost always a degree of wonderment and surprise is expressed when some new facet is revealed.

No facts cause more astonishment amongst newcomers than the revelation that endowments created many years ago enable ministers, missionaries and full-time workers of the Church of Scotland to enjoy a holiday at the Hydro at very much reduced terms. Indeed, from time to time they have been able to have a fortnight here free of all charges; but those days could not go on indefinitely, and small amounts were asked from the individuals, both to augment the bequests and so that more Church workers could benefit.

For a long period this contribution amounted to 3s. per day from each person—£1 1s. per week—so the rather unkind epithet "guinea-pigs" came to be applied to the beneficiaries.

It may not be generally known that there are three separate funds, all directed towards this kindly purpose, the first of them originating in 1867, before one stone of the Hydro building was laid upon another, a premise that suggests two things; one, that in the middle of last century, Church workers were poorly paid; two, that they were greatly respected in the community for their learning, their devotion to their calling, and for their "cloth".

Whatever the reason, they had friends and patrons among the well-to-do. What is not so clear is the strong attraction stirred up by institutions like the Hydropathic, that drew men of strict God-fearing principles to take a keen interest in its welfare, and to offer large sums of money in pursuance of benefits for the Scottish clergy.

And here, before I detail the three Funds, it should be pointed out clearly that each fund was given for the good of a particular denomination of the Church in Scotland.

Not one of these originally involved the established Church of Scotland.

At the end of April 1867, two months after the first meeting of the Hydropathic Establishment Company, Mr James Smieton, owner of the jute weaving factory at Panmure Works, Carnoustie, in the county now called Angus, wrote to the Board offering to lend, on certain terms, £2000 to the Company. Those terms were that the money had to be invested "on behalf of Free Church Ministers", and the Directors were to grant bond for this sum over the property of the Company. Mr Smieton died before anything could be done, but his son, Thomas A. Smieton, wrote soon after intimating his readiness to carry out his father's proposal.

The early notes of meetings state that the Board could not see their way to grant a bond on the property but would give a 5 per cent. debenture, the yearly proceeds of which could be applied as Mr Smieton desired. This did not suit Mr Smieton, and the minutes do not make any further mention of this matter until 1901, when it is quite obvious that the Smieton Fund was in operation.

This earliest fund is still helping to give ministers and others holidays at the Hydro, but it is administered wholly by the Church of Scotland.

The events leading finally to its establishment clearly indicate the determination of the family to see their father's wishes carried out. Once the Hydropathic Directors had made it clear that they would not grant their property as security, the family invested £2000 in the Caledonian and the North British Railway Companies stock, and arranged for the fund to be administered by trustees appointed by the General Assembly of the Free Church of Scotland.

The declaration of trust explains that the proceeds from the investments are to enable ordained ministers to retire for a few weeks from their duties, for the benefit of their health, and that preference was to be given to ministers whose income did not exceed £200 per annum. This document goes on to say:

"In respect that a Hydropathic Establishment has lately been erected near Crieff . . . and that so long as it shall be conducted to the satisfaction of the said Managers, the recipients of the Grants shall be required to reside as Boarders there for such period as the Grants, after deducting Travelling Expenses, shall permit."

The first meeting of the Managers took place in the offices of the Free Church in Edinburgh on 20th January 1870, those present being Sir Henry Wellwood Moncrieff, Bart., Moderator of the General Assembly of that Church; George Meldrum and Thomas Smieton.

A sum of £100 was available in the first year, and advertisements were to be inserted in the *Dundee Advertiser*, the *North British Advertiser* and the *Free Church Record*, asking for applications from ministers in the Synod of Angus and Mearns. If there were a lack of applications from that Synod then the Synod of Fife was to be included.

The Smieton Fund is still managed in this way, extending throughout Scotland, and principally for the benefit of Ministers with lower stipends.

The Paton Fund

About the time of the opening of the Establishment in August 1868, Mr David Paton, one of the original directors, said he was "disposed to increase his interest in or grant a loan to the Company, and was desirous to send United Presbyterian ministers and missionaries to the Establishment to receive Board and Treatment free of charge to them". He offered to lend £4000 and enquired the rate of interest to be given on loans and what abatement from the regular charges would be allowed him in consideration of his sending to the Establishment many parties who might influence others.

In answer to this, "the Directors agreed on 5 per cent. interest on loans secured by Debentures over the Property and Revenue of the Company, and allowed him a rebatement of 15 per cent. from 52s. 6d. (single) and 87s. 6d.

(double), the Rates or 'Terms' charged to the Public for the time being. This tentative measure to run for one year".

Mr Paton added another £2000 to this in 1877, the interest, of course, to be applied for the benefit of workers in the United Presbyterian Church, and terms exactly as before. Three years later he asked for repayment of the £2000 and intimated that he was transferring his bond of £4000, which stood in the name of trustees, to his daughter, Miss Agnes Paton, to be held by her absolutely.

In 1885 Miss Paton married Dr Meikle and the records show that she then began to take an even greater interest in the Hydro and the welfare of some of its visitors. She acquired 50 more shares that year and at the same time, although Dr Meikle had informed the Board that her bond of £4000 had been discharged, she indicated that she was still anxious to continue the scheme for the benefit of U.P. Church ministers. The Directors, therefore, approved proposals to induce a larger number of ministers to come to the House during the slacker winter months. Here is the first indication of bringing more beneficiaries in the off season, which was to be developed later on.

While the benefactions went on without a break, some changes took place in the actual source. For instance, in 1895 the Directors agreed to sell 80 shares at such price and terms as "they consider beneficial for the Company in reduction of debt".

To do this they had to hold a special meeting of shareholders and at it a letter was read from Mrs Meikle offering to purchase the 80 shares for £3000 or £37 10s. per share, ex dividend. She added that they would be transferred to trustees to be named by her, who would for 23 years hold them and apply the dividends in payment of board and residence of Protestant ministers, missionaries, Christian workers and others. The minute of agreement gave Mrs Meikle the sole right to make such rules and regulations as to admission and period of residence.

The sum expended under the Paton Fund that financial year was £223 13s. 1d. Before the stipulated period of 23 years had expired as it was due to do in 1918, Mrs Meikle put up additional money.   This was in 1910 and a note in the minutes for some three years later states:

"Of the £7,050 of 'unsecured' debt owing by the Company, it was agreed to give 6 Debentures for £1,000 each, leaving £1,050 still owing by the Company to Mrs Agnes Meikle."

On the death of Mrs Meikle in 1919 it was necessary to issue new debentures to the beneficiaries under her will for the remaining £4000 still owing by the Company.

From this point, onwards the Paton Fund has been operated smoothly alongside the Meikle Fund, the same Trustees being responsible for both.

THE MEIKLE TRUST

The Meikle Trust is the largest of the three Trusts.   The Smieton and Paton Funds, in the early years of the Company, did a great deal of good work, but when William Meikle presented his fund, in 1901, the numbers who could take advantage of those benefactions were more than doubled. In recent years over 800 individuals have annually enjoyed the benefits of these Funds.

The first mention of William Meikle's intention was given by Dr Meikle at a Board meeting on 22nd September 1900, when he announced that a very generous arrangement was being made by their co-Director to give the benefits of the Establishment to the ministers, missionaries and Christian workers of the United Free Church, by creating a Trust and providing very ample funds for this purpose.   At the A.G.M. on 4th May 1901, Mr Meikle's act received prominence, and it was further said that it would give the privilege of a fortnight's residence "on very favourable terms".

At that meeting it was proposed that the Meikle and Paton Funds should be worked in concert, and that is the position to this day.

It is said that blessings never come singly and that, certainly, happened at the meeting in September 1900.

The Chairman (Dr Meikle) also intimated that Mrs Meikle had presented the Company with the Pipe Organ now erected in the Drawing room, which had already been found very helpful at Worship and for Organ Recitals of which a number have already been given. The Directors have to thank her for her gift. With their permission, Mrs Meikle also proposes to be at the expense of removing and fitting up the old organ in a Mission Church at Coalsnaughton, near Alloa, which permission was cordially given.

Mrs Meikle's gift is still found very helpful at the Sunday evening and other services held in the drawing room. Further, I have been told that the old organ given to the mission at Coalsnaughton is still functioning.

William Meikle died in 1905, and while alive he ran the fund himself, so there are no minutes for the first four years. As mentioned, two weeks constituted the holiday stretch in ordinary circumstances, but this could be extended at the discretion of the Manager.

In 1911 the Trustees decided to spend £460 out of revenue, but this grew steadily by £50, sometimes by £100 per annum, until in 1919 the figure jumped to £1200 and in 1920 soared to over £2000, which held for some years, with one or two exceptions when more money was available. Throughout most of this period the beneficiaries received free residence for a fortnight if their salaries were less than £500. Over that amount they paid three shillings a day, and when money grew tighter that became a general charge.

Despite the fact that the terms of all three bequests included "Christian workers", the wives of ministers were not, for many years, allowed to benefit; but in 1919 this question arose and it was decided that the lady of the manse *was* a Christian worker and eligible. Two years later that decision was reversed but within another two years it was granted again, and to-day wives are welcomed in their own right as workers for the Church. Following the Union in 1929 of the Church of Scotland and the United Free Church, the question of ministers of the United Free Church (Continuing) being allowed to participate in these Funds was raised, but Counsel turned that down. Counsel, when asked about ministers' wives participating, had agreed that it was right for them to do so.

In 1927 draft regulations drawn up for administering the

Meikle Fund stated that each beneficiary should pay four shillings a day, these terms not being available during holiday periods. A medical certificate meant free residence. All ministers had to be prepared to conduct morning and evening services if asked. The following year the daily charge dropped to 3s. 6d. per day and in 1931 the stipend (salary) limit, below which ministers were given a fortnight's residence free of charge, dropped to £400. By 1935, three shillings again became the charge, and in the event of there being more applicants than funds permitted, the Trustees reserved the right of selection. The fortnight could not be broken into more than two periods. Similar conditions attached to the Paton Fund, with the added proviso that those who were entitled to benefit from the Meikle Fund were excluded from the Paton Fund.

During the Second World War, when the House was full of Army troops, the Trustees continued to give opportunities to those eligible for a holiday at Crieff, by booking accommodation for them in private houses in the town. Anyone who needed medical attention simply applied to one of the general practitioners in the district who sent in their bill to the Trustees.

New regulations issued in 1952 cut the length of stay from fourteen days to ten and a minimum of five days, which is what holds to-day. The charges to individuals went up between 1961 and 1962 from £2 12s. 6d. in the low season and £3 13s. 6d. in May and October, to £3 13s. 6d. and £4 14s. 6d. respectively—a subsidy of approximately £8 8s. and £10 10s. per week.

One of the Directors of the Hydropathic Company has always been a Trustee of the Meikle Fund. Dr Gordon Meikle succeeded the Rev. Dr. J. H. Leckie in 1924. Then came Dr Joe Leckie and Mr Gordon Leckie. Mr John Leckie succeeded his father. The other trustees are:— Mr R. W. Campbell, Ayr, chairman; Mr J. D. S. Miller, Crieff; Mr S. L. Drysdale, Crieff; Mr J. M. Robertson, Crieff, and Sheriff A. M. Prain, Crieff.

Many expressions of gratitude are received from beneficiaries and their wives by the trustees for the facilities offered by these funds and the care with which they are managed. This is shown by the willingness of ministers to take morning prayers after breakfast, or the Sunday evening service. The same spirit of willingness to help, it should be remarked here, is seen in the ministers of the churches in and around Crieff, who voluntarily take the Sunday evening services during the weeks when no resident minister is available.

The unwary might expect a solemn quietude to settle over the House when the great majority of guests are ministers and their wives. Such an idea is quite erroneous, as an extract from one of Mrs Modjesky's letters shows.

"All my recollections of the Hydro are of the fun I had there— tennis tournaments, dances, and the hilarious charades my uncle, George Duncan, and I were involved in one year, after the crowds were gone and a group of ministers decided to enliven a dull Sunday evening! Looking back, I realise that those men of the Cloth had a holy joy in life that less Christian people never know."

The Rev. Dr J. Bulloch, of Peebles, was sitting in the billiard room one evening when a man entered.

"Nice to get away from all those damned parsons. The place is swarming with them. What do you do?" asked the man.

Dr Bulloch, who was in 'mufti', said guardedly, "I'm in the spirit trade."

"Oh, that's interesting," said his companion. "I've a pub in Leith. What's your firm?"

"I'm in the Church of Scotland."

Remember what the Epistle to the Hebrews says: Be not forgetful to entertain strangers, for thereby some have entertained angels unawares.

The benefits of the Meikle and Paton Trusts are not all one-sided, as the ministers and their wives help to keep the Hydro busy during the quieter months, and there is a notably happy atmosphere when groups of them get together and exchange their latest experiences and jokes.

STAFF RECORDS

"Well done, good and faithful servant."
The Gospel of St. Matthew

Throughout its long history the Hydropathic has been fortunate in its servants. And in that word "servants" I include all, from Dr Thomas Meikle downwards. An old proverb says "Like will to like" and this certainly applies to personalities, so that it would seem that the Management of the Establishment have found staff to match themselves. A contented and hard-working staff forms the highest tribute to employer and conditions of work.

From the day of opening in August 1868, and backed by the nucleus of a dozen or more servants and artisans brought from Aberdeen, a reliable band of almost 50 came into service. They were well looked after and reviews of the pay-roll took place regularly, Dr Meikle keeping his finger on the pulse of conditions as well as on the character of each individual. Little escaped him and his assessment of people seldom proved wrong.

No one would have been more delighted than he to learn at this juncture in the story of the Hydro, that the Directors have rewarded a number of employees for their years of service to the Company; notably five who, still serving, have a total of 155 years' work in and around the House. They are:—Alexander Carle, in charge of garaging and Hydro 'bus (43 years); Andrew McKay, head painter (37 years); Miss M. G. Stenhouse, office staff (32 years); Miss Nan Robertson, housemaid (25 years); George McInnes, head gardener (22 years); Frank Dunbar, porter (21 years).

Back in the early days the first names of any of the staff to appear in the records are those of John Cook and his wife, Ann, who moved to Crieff with Dr Meikle from Aberdeen. At the end of October 1875, Mrs Cook died, and after that John Cook became very unsettled. He wrote resigning four months later, was persuaded to stay on, departed to another job a year later, and returned soon after, his new master having died. Dr Meikle could always find him something to do, and the last entry in minutes of 1882 shows that he was being allowed to live in the House, except for three or four summer months, at a charge of three shillings a day, less one month free.

The second name to appear, and one which is still spoken of with a high degree of respect by those who know something of the Hydro's story, is that of James Lamb. Engaged as a bathman and joiner in 1871, he had attained the rank of Master of Works before he died at the age of 67, still working, in 1912—"after 41 years' faithful and intelligent service", state the minutes. His ambit ranged over the whole of the Company's activities, for it seemed that there was nothing he could not undertake successfully, whether it were the widening of the dining hall by a foot or more at each side, the repair of the dam in 1910, or the simple repair of a door lock.

If Lamb was a character in the out-of-doors, James Caw formed his counterpart inside the Establishment. In his little book, *Reminiscences of Forty Years on the Staff of a Hydro— 1873–1913*, Mr Caw relates some of his experiences while acting as clerk, then house steward, but in fact, there was a gap in his services of 12 years when he suffered serious nervous depression and a complete breakdown in health, between 1896 and 1908. At that time the Directors offered to pay for a sea voyage to the Cape, but he refused and went to Mentone, in the south of France.

A former illness brought Caw into touch with Dr Meikle. He was a Crieff laddie who, after serving his apprenticeship in the Central Bank of Scotland in Perth, joined the Bank of Liverpool in 1862. Prospects for him there were bright, but he had to leave in 1868 on account of his health. Ultimately he managed to stagger, with the aid of crutches, as far as the Hydro where he received a course of baths and some office work to do. He came on to the staff in 1873 and three years later became House Steward in succession to Mr Cook, the minute-book stating that he had filled the post of assistant house steward so efficiently that he was

PLATE 7

Members of the Staff, 1986

(Unfortunately some members of the staff could not be included in this photograph)

PLATE 8

Dr. J. P. Leckie

Sir T. M. Knox

Dr. T. G. Meikle

J. R. Donaldson

Wm. Meikle

W. G. Leckie

promoted, his salary being £100 a year with board, lodging and washing. For his intromissions and the faithful discharge of his duties he had to find security in the sum of £400.

Thereafter, until he broke down in health, his work was recognised at regular intervals by increases in salary, and when he went on sick leave he had reached £300 per annum. In 1883 he married one of the girls in the Hydro office, and it seems as if she had continued to work there for in 1889 the Directors agreed "to give Mr and Mrs Caw a larger bonus in proportion to the success of the Establishment".

Both were favourites with the visitors and deservedly so, for they were helpful and knowledgeable, and he, to judge by his writings, possessed a wonderful store of tales, religious and cautionary, and all in the idiom of last century.

Kindly reference was made at a Board meeting at the time of his death in 1914.

Since the year of opening, the Hydro has had dozens of loyal and faithful servants, but for length of service the palm must go to David Stenhouse who came on to the payroll before James Lamb, though the minutes do not give the year. His name appears as "Coachman" under the Hydropathic's list of servants in the Census of 1871, and in 1909 a paragraph in the records states:

"It is about 40 years since David Stenhouse became Bus-man to this Company, so it was agreed to present him with £40 in recognition of his faithful service."

He must, therefore, have been taken on in 1869 or 1870. That entry is not all, for the month of May 1920, brings this:

"Chairman brought up question of a donation to Mr Stenhouse (busman) and it was agreed to give him a present of £50 on his golden wedding."

That means that he must have been about 50 years in the employment of the Company. He was, for a great many years, the first member of the staff of the Hydro that visitors met, as he was the last they saw, for in his top-hat which bore the legend "HYDRO" round the front, he made an unmistakable figure at Crieff station.

That same census of 1871 gives us some clues to the names of men and women who accompanied Dr Meikle from Aberdeen. It seems highly probable that William Strath (or Straith), born in Kinellar, Aberdeen; John Knox Ironside, from Forres, and Morris Watson, a Chelsea pensioner born in Banffshire, may all have moved with the Doctor. They were all bath attendants, an occupation requiring training and skill which they had probably learned at Loch-Head.

The youngest member of staff at any time was surely James Kidd, post boy in 1871, and aged 12 years.

There must, of course, have been many of the women servants who stayed for long periods with the Company, but the record for the early part of the Hydro's existence goes to Mary Thomson, bath attendant and later housemaid. She must have held a very humble post, for when James Caw gets a rise of £40 per annum, Mary gets £4. On leaving her job at Martinmas 1895, however, the Directors made a gesture proving her worth and their generosity, for they awarded her £2 for each year of service—twice the amount they were in the habit of giving—and she received £55. The Census tells us that she was born in 1841 at Monquhitter, in the Turriff district of Aberdeenshire, which suggests that she, too, had come south with Dr Meikle in 1868. The staff at the time of the Census included two other women from Monquhitter, four others also from Aberdeenshire, two from Banffshire and one from Forres.

An echo of the 'Eighties and 'Nineties of last century sounded in 1927, for the Board considered recognising the long service of two men, Francis Watt and James Rigg. The former, a bathman, was settled, with wife, son and daughter, in one of the cottages in 1881, and he died in service in 1927, so that he had been for at least 46 years with the Company, and his widow received something in recognition of that fact. Details about James Rigg are even more sketchy. He retired on pension in 1927, but when he joined the staff is not shown. From the careful, tidy and numerous notes he made on the installation and working of both the gas-driven and water-power electric plants, he shows himself to have been painstaking and industrious. He came as a plumber but obviously enjoyed looking after the electrical machinery, for he left two copies of detailed instructions and duties for the attendant, whoever that might be, at the power house.

Other names of persons who spent long years at the Hydro include John Simpson, gardener, induced to retire after 24 years, 1873–97; James McDonald, joiner, 1880–1914; Alfred MacIntyre, clerk and cashier, 1888–1917; Miss Hoy, office staff—many years till her death in 1933; Andrew Smith, head gardener—many years till his death in 1933; George Reid, gardener, who began on 1st May 1907, to take the daily meteorological readings, still kept by Mr McInnes —many years service; and Miss Robertson, assistant house-keeper, 1905–33. Miss Watt, who was in charge of Dallerie Laundry for 20 years, resigned in 1921.

To many guests of a more recent generation the name of Miss Mary B. Ewing was as well known as any on the Hydro roll.

Beginning work in 1913, the year in which Dr Thomas Meikle died, Miss Ewing saw the effects of two world wars on the Hydro and on the way of life of those who came to the Hydro. She began work when horse-drawn carriages and buses were the normal means of transport; when the dining room had a few long tables and guests moved up as others departed so that it became the height of ambition in some to reach the top of the table in the "House of Lords", as the dining room annex came to be called. That, of course, meant either a long stay or a lot of luck.

She left when the only horses to be seen were the ponies in Mrs Barbara Leckie's riding stables at the Hydro, and when the only long table in the dining room appeared on those special days when the Chef's cold buffet dishes were displayed.

"The first motor bus was a great event," she told me two years ago, "and a great boon to the visitors, allowing them to get up and down to the shops in Crieff. It was all very well for those who could walk, but the climb up the hill proved too much for many who were invalids. Those who came for treatment stayed much longer than they do nowadays. Some of them—perhaps about a dozen—could hardly leave their rooms, and meals had to be taken up to them.

"At that time, too, there were coal fires in all bedrooms and coal had to be carried up every day by the porters. All the girls lived in, and the housemaids had to help the waitresses in the dining room. But I saw hot and cold water laid on to the bedrooms and gas fires put in, and these improvements made a big difference." Miss Ewing, before becoming hostess, had charge of the house staff and also of the stillroom.

A delightful slant on life in the Hydro comes from Mrs Modjesky, who writes:

"There were the occasions when a certain lady guest, who laboured under the delusion that she could sing, would perform at the Sunday evening concerts, and even Miss Ewing, whose dignity and poise were second only to the late Queen Mary's, would have to make a hasty exit, and we young people would have to crawl behind the sofas with our handkerchiefs stuffed in our mouths."

And what of the staff of later days? Miss Ewing, of course, spanned both world wars and is remembered by many of those who have had Crieff Hydro as a focal point in holiday plans throughout their lives.

Of the staff at the time of writing (1967), the man with the longest service is Alec Carle. He became an employee of the company in 1925, and recalls many amusing episodes of 40 years ago when, he says, the visitors had to be right canny in their approach to the bathmen, because if they annoyed these experts, they were liable to get a douche of icy cold water when they least expected it.

Mr Carle tells a story of an even earlier bathman who was blunt and forthright and said to the visitor who, about to leave, stated that he felt very much better for the course of treatment, "Well, I wouldn't know about that, but I ken ye're a lot cleaner than ye were when ye cam'."

Three years after Carle—I am sure most visitors think

that is his first name, for that is all he gets from them—
came Douglas McLennan, formerly head porter and now
retired and living in the cottage near the eastern entrance
to the grounds. A native of Banchory, he had the Aber-
donian's pawky humour, but a firm hand, as rowdy children
around the entrance hall, ballroom and winter garden soon
found out. Not that he did not enjoy seeing the young folk
enjoying themselves. I can remember him helping a
teenager to carry a high pair of steps to the verge of the
ballroom floor so that the lad could take a photo of the "tea
gang" of about 30 sitting at the righthand wall as one enters
the ballroom. Mr McLennan held the steps while the
photo was taken. He retired in 1965, after 37 years' service.

Since the appointment of the first Chef as distinct from a
Cook, a change that took place in 1907, there have apparently been only three chefs—Gillies A. Calazel, 1907 to
1922; David Sibbald, 1922 to 1939; and Alexander Mac-
Gregor, who joined in 1949 before the Hydro re-opened after
de-requisitioning, and is still in command. Trained at
Fortingall Hotel, Perthshire, he afterwards gained his
"Cordon Bleu" in Paris. On the outbreak of war in 1939
he went to the Black Watch and after training found himself
at the Army School of Cookery at Troon, where, among
other adventures, he met his wife. His next move was to a
Messing Officers' Training Centre outside Edinburgh.
When he was demobilised he worked at the Invercauld
Arms, Braemar, then at Loch Awe Hotel, in Argyll, before
coming to the Hydro.

"It was a lucky day for the Hydro when a Mr Gavin, a tea
traveller, who had been calling at the Hydro for many years,
recommended a chef he knew—Alexander MacGregor, whose
enthusiasm, cheerfulness and resource in the face of almost
insurmountable obstacles were a tonic to all those who were
battling frantically to keep the opening date at Easter 1949. To
give a much-needed boost to our morale, and to let the guests
see that there was one member of the Establishment who could
give the professional touch, he would appear in the front hall
and walk briskly to the main office wearing immaculate uniform,
complete to the top of his well-starched hat. This must have

been a reassuring sight for the guests, some of whom had had the rather unnerving experience of being ushered into a bedroom minus a bed or a wardrobe . . . The skill and artistry that go to the making of his Christmas cake—a model of the new Forth road bridge, or a church with steeple, all lighted by electricity, have to be seen and tasted to be appreciated."

So writes one lady who has known the Hydro for many years.

The senior members of the kitchen staff give a fine air of stability amongst the workers in that sphere, for George Howell, the second chef, came in 1949, and Edward Stewart and Hans Protze, third chef and baker respectively, in 1951.

I have mentioned in that section dealing with electricity, that Dr Meikle would not allow the wires to be enclosed in any way, and this lasted for some years, until the cables were placed between long, narrow, hollowed-out spars of wood which were then fastened to the walls. Ultimately, when rewiring had to be done, it was undertaken by the excellent Sandy Mitchell, who is still remembered affectionately by some of the older people.

Sandy's assistant was another worthy, Donald Sutherland, who spent forty years in the service of the Hydro. His wife acted as a cook in the Hydro for a long period before 1939, being responsible for the special diets which Dr Meikle provided for his patients.

Donald, brought up in Caithness, left home with this advice from his father when he started work in Dundee.

"Firstly, never forget your prayers, pray every night. If you are in trouble or difficulty, ask for help and guidance, and if it is for your good, the Lord will grant it. Be obedient to those in authority over you, never answer back—be willing to oblige and help others. Avoid bad company . . . If you find a good chum, stick to him. . . .

"Keep away from bad girls, never be seen with anyone that you would be ashamed to introduce to your Mother. Never tell lies, better tell the truth and stand the consequences than be put down as a liar . . . Strive after knowledge. Knowledge is power. Treat your employer's gear as if it was your own."

These proved the guiding principles by which Donald and other faithful servants of the Company worked and died in its service.

The care of the staff has always been a preoccupation with the Directors, Dr Meikle, of course, leading the way, and it was that spirit of concern for their welfare that led the Board, as long ago as 1883, to formulate a savings scheme.

"In order to encourage the servants to take an interest in the welfare of the Establishment, the Directors proposed to offer the servants the privilege of lending to the Company their savings at a rate of 1 per cent. less than the Dividend and Bonus for the year."

As the Company was paying seven per cent. with a bonus of one per cent. at this time, it was a good opportunity for the staff to invest whatever they could save. As already indicated this scheme ran until 1942 when the deposits were repaid. After the outbreak of war in 1939, the Hydro being filled with troops, all dividends to shareholders ceased, but the Board went on paying the servant depositors four per cent. interest.

In 1950, a year after the post-war re-opening of the Establishment, it was decided that, in the event of the Company paying a dividend the staff would be paid a global sum as a bonus. This, by the end of that year, amounted to over £800, and two years later the auditor was asked to go into the matter of superannuation for the staff.

Since then the staff bonus has grown until, at the present day, it is in the region of £2500. There is also a pension and life assurance scheme, and as recently as 1962 this was extended to give an additional life assurance benefit for all male members, the whole cost being borne by the Company.

The whole staff, including the farms and the laundry, numbers about 150, and except among the younger element —waitresses and housemaids—little change takes place. Mrs Annie G. Crichton, who began work in the Hydro in 1918 and is a night nurse there still, recently described her first job. She was a house-table maid, which meant doing two jobs—housemaid and waitress—and the hours were from seven in the morning to ten o'clock at night. For that she was paid eight shillings a week and, though they got time off every second day, they had no recognised day off. There was no idling. For all that, the Hydro was considered a very good place to work. She recalled a time when the young guests had a big table to themselves in the dining room and had great fun together.

The bathmaids of old—Sarah, Lizzie, Nellie and Edith—had to undertake any nursing that was necessary, and diets were served if required.

One of the highlights of the year for many of the servants was the "Staff Party", when guests put on white aprons and, while the ladies acted as waitresses the men served the joints at the side table. A day or two after this event a Christmas party was given for the children of employees, and each of the young people received a new sixpence from Mrs Meikle. Both parties still go on and are much enjoyed; and the sixpence has grown into a shilling, an apple, an orange, and a 'poke' of sweeties.

And now, in the spring of 1967, the staff have their own social club, with quiz nights, "record" nights, and dances, in go-ahead, modern fashion.

HAIL! AND FARE WELL

Crieff Hydro. Here we are, back where we began, in the warmth and comfort of this great Establishment of contentment and happiness.

In those periods that bring swarms of holiday-makers there comes an air of excitement arising out of constant activity and high endeavour to fit in as many pleasurable moments as possible. For years now the high seasons have brought great enjoyment with them, and the old building seems to rejoice, too, and to become young again; for, as it fitted into the pattern of hydropathy in its youth, so it has been adapted to each era as it has come and passed.

Not that it has lost the rare power to soothe, to calm, to heal, that Dr Meikle breathed into it all through the half century that he had lived with it, mentally and physically. Do not for an instant imagine this magic potion is lost.

Visit the Hydro during one of the low months. All the old potent atmosphere is still there; all the peace, all the quiet—the spacious quiet—that exudes from the surroundings, from the very sunshine itself, can be summed up only by the words of St. Matthew

". . . and ye shall find rest unto your souls."

No wonder that the firm discipline of the hand in the velvet glove, as practised by Dr Meikle, so appealed to all in search of peace, in the sterner days of 100 years ago.

This atmosphere of the Hydropathic has even inspired guests to write poetry about it; to extol its virtues in books, in the press and in public speech; even to form little groups the better to enjoy one another's company. One such "club" went so far as to produce a typewritten booklet entitled "The Crieff Annual". Surely innocent amusement and good-will towards the fellowship which Strathearn House creates could go no further.

The story of the first 45 years of this remarkable and distinguished Establishment is to a great extent the story of Thomas Henry Meikle. He died in 1913, but his life's work goes on—a lasting memorial.

The future lies ahead and holds we know not what destiny for any of us. So long, however, as the spirit of Thomas Meikle is felt within these walls and around the Directors' table, so long will persons of cheerful and earnest qualities enjoy the happy aura that surrounds

CRIEFF HYDRO

FINIS

APPENDIX I

SIX CHAIRMEN IN A HUNDRED YEARS

Should anyone cavil at the biographies of the Chairmen of the Company being put into an appendix, the answer is that an appendix, like the postcript to a letter, contains the most important message of all.

In the space of its 100 years' existence the Strathearn Hydropathic Establishment Company, Ltd., has had six chairmen—Charles W. Anderson, 19 years; William Meikle, 10 years; Thomas Meikle, 17 years; Gordon Meikle, 31 years; Joseph P. Leckie, 7 years; and J. R. Donaldson, 16 years and still going strong.

Before looking at these men, let us glance again at Thomas Henry Meikle. Throughout this story the frequent references made to him in the day-to-day life of the Hydro have given a picture of the man, but it is not complete. For example, the treatment which the Company received from Crieff Town Council in its first 25 years would quickly have embittered many men; but Thomas Meikle was not of that calibre. Always thoughtful of other people's welfare, he did not allow snubs to upset him or divert him from good actions.

James Caw, writing in 1913, long after the bitter squabbles over the water supply had ceased, said:

"The Hydro Establishment has never been credited by the 'man in the street' as having been of much benefit to Crieff. It has never been popular with the inhabitants, and why this should be is difficult to understand. The amount of money disbursed in Crieff (Crieff alone) from the Hydro office is now over £12,000 annually."

Despite this unfortunate attitude in the town, Dr and Mrs Meikle offered Crieff a hospital, on which work (according to Caw) had actually begun, when the Council refused the gift. The plans for this hospital are still in the possession of the Hydro. Later, Dr Meikle presented the Strathearn Institute to the town, and, only weeks before his death, made over the Knock of Crieff to the Council for the towns-people. The local Inspector of Poor told James Caw that, but for the food allowed by Dr Meikle to be given away at the kitchen door of the Hydro, many poor families in the town would have starved.

Hydropathic Establishment.—We understand that the Directors of this Establishment have again resumed their most laudable and praiseworthy object of relieving the destitute during the most severe months of winter, when work in this locality is very scarce, by distributing a supply of excellent soup, twice a week, from their kitchen, to a large number of infirm and deserving poor.

So wrote the editor of the *Strathearn Herald* on 19th November 1870. I suspect that Dr Meikle did this on his own initiative. The Directors may have known about it, for he would not attempt to hide it, but he had a habit of doing things like this without telling anyone. Caw says that delicate students, needing a longer stay at the Hydro, got it by Dr Meikle handing Caw the money out of his own pocket.

Some years before the Directors inaugurated the servants' deposit fund, Dr Meikle had opened a "Savings Bank" for the staff.

Three years after the opening of the Establishment the Board agreed that the Manager should have every facility for taking exercises and that his horse should be kept and tended at the Company's expense; also, that he should take a month's vacation each year when convenient. No further reference to this holiday period is made, and it seems likely that the Doctor never attempted to take any more than a day or two off, now and again. His work was his life.

Mrs Modjesky gives some intimate details about the Meikle family.

'My father was born on 19th Jan. 1864, and went to Morrison's Academy, Crieff, but I do not know what years I do know that he was a resident at Beth'lem Hospital and I think Aunt Edith was Matron there for some time (possibly 1905 to 1912). My father wanted to specialise in neurology and it was a sacrifice for him to return to Crieff, as, according to Dr Theo Hyslop, he was very gifted".

Talking of her grandfather and Agnes Paton, his second wife, she says:

"When they became engaged he gave her a bracelet set with six stones, denoting the six step-children she was about to acquire. She was so fond and proud of my father [one of the step-children] that, when she visited him in Edinburgh she forbade her maid to tell anyone she was not his real mother. My father's only brother, James Reay, died of meningitis at Blair Lodge School, aged 16.

"It is too bad, from your point of view, that the Meikles were not American; they are so family-tree minded. The Scots are content to stand on their own merits."

Agnes Paton, as described by Mrs Mickel, Crieff, mother of one of the present Directors, sounded a very queenly and dignified person. One striking detail—she often wore a dress of ruby red velvet with a ruby ring to match. She was, in fact, an extremely kind and good woman.

Mrs Mickel, recalling Edith Patricia Meikle, said she was very go-ahead; into everything and always ready for high jinks. She married a cousin, William Meikle, and lived a good deal in London.

WILLIAM MEIKLE

Actuary

For as long as the Hydropathic exists so will the name of William Meikle be blest. This is a second William Meikle, a cousin of the two doctors, Thomas and William, but a good deal older than either of them, for he was born in 1815, the year of the Battle of Waterloo.

The Hydro is full of surprises, and only a matter of months ago I met Bailie A. B. Mackay, Glasgow, on holiday there, who told me he had been trained in Glasgow Savings Bank by William Meikle. Here was a link covering more than 150 years. An aura of longevity seems to be cast by the Hydro on many of its favoured sons and daughters. William

Meikle lived to be 90. David Paton, another director and
benefactor to the Scottish Church, lived to be 90; and
Charles W. Anderson, chairman for the first 19 years of the
Company died in 1901 aged 90. Dr Meikle himself was 79
when he died.

William Meikle is noted for two outstanding contributions
to the happiness of many thousands of people during his
lifetime. The one directly connected with the Hydropathic
is the Meikle Fund which he instituted in 1900. The other
developed from his life's work. After leaving school he
entered a law office as an apprentice. He seems, however,
to have been keen on figures and must have concentrated
on this subject in his younger days, for when he was 25
years of age he entered the National Security Savings Bank
in Glasgow as accountant. Promotion came rapidly and in
1849 he was appointed actuary, a position which he held
until he was well over 80. In 1900, then in his 85th year,
he was presented with an illuminated address as a mark of
esteem for his enterprise and good management of the Bank.
By that time it had become Glasgow Savings Bank, and
William Meikle had materially assisted in its rise from
deposits of £154,000 in 1849, to £10,000,000 in 1900. This
work proved his second contribution to the happiness of
many. He had also taken an active interest in the "Penny
Bank" movement. For a number of years he was an elder
in Claremont U.F. Church.

In 1898, when he was 83, and still keeping an eye on the
Bank, he published a small booklet on the history of the
Savings Bank of Glasgow. As could be expected, coming
from such a man, it consists very largely of tables of the
financial position at various times in the second half of last
century.

This preoccupation with money and figures apparently
ran in the family, for William's half-brother, Christopher
Meikle, who lived in Portobello, Edinburgh, for many
years and was for a short time a director of the Hydropathic
Company, was the actuary of the Edinburgh Savings Bank.
It is worth mentioning here that at the annual general
meeting of the Hydro Company on 6th May 1899, there

were five Meikles present.   Doctors Thomas and Gordon, William and Christopher, and the Rev. Gilbert Meikle, from Inveraray.   It was at this meeting that Christopher became a director, but he retired in favour of Charles D. Ritchie, in May 1900.

At the general meeting of 13th May 1904, ill health caused William to retire from the Board.   He had been a director for 37 years and was the last of the original Board still alive. Dr Gordon Meikle was appointed a director in his stead. Once he was able to take matters in Glasgow more easily, William Meikle bought a house in Crieff called Dalmhor, which is situated just outside the main gate into the Hydro grounds.   Here he and his older sister, Jane, settled down and took, if possible, an even greater interest in the activities in and around Strathearn House, finding, in the last five years of his life, an engrossing plaything in the form of his fund for the benefit of ministers.

Latterly he and Jane lived much in the Hydro, but it was at Dalmhor, on 9th September 1905, full of contentment and of years, that William Meikle passed to his long rest.

His sister died in 1909, aged 96.

Charles W. Anderson
Chairman 1867–1886

At least three of the provisional directors took the chair at early meetings between February and May 1867, and it was not until a meeting in September that Mr Charles W. Anderson was appointed Chairman of the now established Board.

The firm of Robert Anderson and Co., commission merchants and agents, were in business in Gayfield Square, Edinburgh, not less than 35 years before Charles William Anderson, a son of the founder, became interested in Crieff Hydropathic.   In business, as circumstances changed so he altered the scope of his work, which suggests a mind prepared to move with the times.

By 1862 he had moved out of the city to a house called Ashton, at Eskbank, Dalkeith, and it was here he lived at the time of purchasing shares in the Hydro Company.

To control successfully, as he did, the Board of a new
company over its first 19 years, when all the glamour of
novelty had evaporated and the worries of completely
unknown situations kept casting ugly shadows; to control a
group of men, each having his own flourishing business and
so almost certainly his individual views on how this new
venture should be run, must surely point to a great deal of
firmness, a vast amount of tact, and a great faith in Thomas
Meikle. Once more, the minutes show an astonishing degree
of responsibility placed in the hands of the Chairman and the
Manager. Together they were left to deal with many
thorny problems, and how smoothly they did so speaks well
for both of them.

By 1885, in poor health, he gave up the chairmanship and
finally resigned in April 1889. He died on 24th January
1901, at 15 Hatton Place, Grange, Edinburgh.

Dr T. Gordon Meikle
Managing Director

To fill the vacancy on the Board caused by the death of
Mr Paton, the directors at a meeting of 1st October 1890,
appointed Dr T. Gordon Meikle, son of Dr Thomas Gordon,
born in Aberdeen, had come to Crieff when he was about
four years of age, and naturally would be put to school at
Morrison's Academy which had opened some eight years
before the Hydropathic began to function. The young lad
grew into a fine athlete and a good tennis player.

From school Gordon Meikle went to Edinburgh University
in 1882 to take a medical degree and he graduated in 1887,
when he was 23 years old. The next three years were spent
in acquiring knowledge and experience in different parts of
the country. As stated, he was appointed a director of the
Company in 1890, but when the semi-jubilee of the founding
of the Hydro came along, in 1892, the directors made
another change.

"Dr Meikle now Manager and Medical Superintendent for
25 years, and as the business of the Company is now very large,
the House being frequently crowded with visitors and patients,

the Directors feel that the time has come when something should be done to strengthen Dr Meikle's hands and relieve him from care and over-anxiety especially in the medical department, they therefore propose that his son, Dr T. Gordon Meikle should be appointed to assist him in the various duties of his office. Dr Gordon has had a thorough university education, and is an M.B., C.M., of Edinburgh and has had much experience and training in hospitals and asylums both in Glasgow and London."

That statement appears in the report to be submitted to the annual general meeting later that day (4th May 1892), and when the A.G.M. took place Christopher Meikle moved that Dr Thomas H. Meikle be elected a director in room of Dr T. Gordon Meikle, who was due to retire, and this was agreed. Dr Gordon then became assistant to his father at a salary of £200 a year.

Thereafter he settled down to the job, gradually absorbing the whole atmosphere of the Establishment; getting to know every individual who worked with him in the House, and all the artisans in the grounds and on the farm; treating the invalids and other guests with courteous consideration and becoming a second "Dr Meikle".

Gordon Meikle seemed destined to succeed notable men in his progress through life. First, he took over the seat on the Board left vacant by the death of David Paton; then, having filled the office of assistant to his father for 12 years, he returned to the Board when William Meikle, now aged 89, decided to retire on account of the state of his health. That was in May 1904, and in 1913, after his father's death, he became medical superintendent and managing director. How well he fitted into that niche is shown by his years in command, and also by the tributes paid.

At his death the Rev. Dr Ferguson, of the North Church, Crieff, who was a trustee of the Meikle Fund, said:

"Dr Gordon Meikle was ever a gentleman, in the noblest sense of that often misused word. A certain reserve of manner and an instinctive aversion from effusive speech, gave to his invariable and impartial courtesy a peculiar charm. Yet he had a gift of terse and incisive speech which he could use with devastating effect when occasion called for it. He had that indefinable quality—is it just a considerateness for others and a genuine appreciation of their good qualities?—that won the hearts of those, who, for any length of time, were in his service, so that they came to love him for his gentle, firm, courteous bearing to one and all.

"He once once asked me to go and talk to a young Australian who had taken ill in the Hydro, and the boy poured out a flood of astonishment that he, a complete stranger to the Hydro, should be treated so kindly by everyone from Dr Meikle downwards."

Miss M. B. Ewing, who is mentioned previously, paid her tribute. "Dr Meikle was very understanding. I never saw him angry in my life."

When Dr Gordon took over after his father's death he was still unmarried, but in 1915, when he was 51, he married Miss Mary Macwhirter, an Edinburgh girl, aged 21, whose father was a silk mercer in the city. There were two daughters, and Mrs Modjesky, the elder, wrote in 1966 from her home in the United States, when she heard that a history of the Hydro was to be compiled. Parts of her letters are quoted elsewhere.

During Gordon Meikle's management a number of vital changes and alterations were made, for modern trends of thought brought modern methods, and he and his fellow Directors were not slow to carry out new lines of work or routine which they knew would be to the benefit of the business and the comfort of their guests. Culcrieff Farm was bought. Garages for the new mode of transport—the motor car—were built. A motor 'bus was bought. Hot and cold water was installed in the bedrooms and vast maintenance works undertaken.

Then the Second World War broke out and the Establishment closed down. With all the ramifications of compensation and maintenance claims flowing on for years, nothing looked like ever being the same again.

In the spring of 1944 Dr Gordon became ill and he died on 30th June, sincerely lamented by a wide circle of friends, acquaintances and the work people of the Hydropathic.

J. REGINALD DONALDSON
Timber Importer

As has been stated in a previous chapter, Mr Reginald Donaldson became a member of the Board at the annual meeting in May 1949, and followed Dr Joseph Leckie in the Chair in February 1952. He is a Director of James Donaldson and Sons, timber importers, Tayport and Leven, in the County of Fife. The firm was founded in 1864 by his grandfather, and deals chiefly in timber from the Baltic.

After his schooling at Merchiston Castle, Edinburgh, he entered the business, but over the years has found time to devote himself to many different outside pursuits. He is a Justice of the Peace and he has given service to Fife Unionist Association. A very keen cricketer, he captained his school 1st XI and later played for Grange Cricket Club and for Fife County. He is a member of the Royal and Ancient Golf Club, St. Andrews, and of the Royal Perthshire Golfing Society.

THE LECKIE FAMILY

The first member of the Leckie family with whom we have contact in this history is Joseph, born in Falkirk in 1826, the son of Joseph Leckie, umbrella manufacturer. After having chosen the Church as a career, he apparently had doubts of his fitness for so high a calling; he graduated, however, and in 1866 received a unanimous call to Ibrox, Glasgow, to serve in a new United Presbyterian church there. Prior to going there he had been at Millport, on the Big Cumbrae, an island in the Firth of Clyde, and there he had sailed a great deal in small boats and yachts. His church beadle (officer) described how he went out for hours: "He went oot for 'oors, just lookin' at the sea an' the sky, thinkin'. He was an awfu' thinkin' body."

He was a noted preacher and received his degree of Doctor of Divinity in 1877, an academic distinction which his son, Joseph Leckie, also achieved, and after his death in January 1889, his son published a book of his sermons which had a considerable vogue 70 years ago. He had been in

M*

poor health for some time before he died and part of the
year 1888 he spent at Crieff Hydro, in which his wife had
shares. Some of these shares passed to young Joseph from
his mother in 1890, and the following year, for the first time,
the name Leckie appears in the list of those attending the
annual general meeting. From that time he regularly
attended the yearly session of shareholders and on the 18th
March 1910, became a member of the Board, a position he
retained until his death in November 1935. He was often
at the Hydro, and Douglas McLennan, formerly head porter,
recalls seeing him playing chess with Dr Gordon Meikle.

His two sons, Joseph Primrose Leckie and William Gordon
Leckie, afterwards became joint Managing Directors of the
Hydropathic and his grandson William Gordon John
Leckie is the present Manager and a Director of the Com-
pany.

Dr Joseph Primrose Leckie
M.B., Ch.B., F.R.C.P.E.

The Rev Dr J. H. Leckie settled down in a U.P., later a
United Free Church of Scotland charge at Cupar, Fife, and
here the family were born. Joe, the oldest son—his middle
name of Primrose was his mother's maiden name—after
school went to St. Andrews University and was there when
war broke out in 1914. He served with the Royal Artillery
in France and on returning to civil life completed his studies
at Edinburgh University, graduating M.B., Ch.B., later
becoming a Fellow of the Royal College of Physicians of
Edinburgh. He was appointed to succeed his father on the
Hydropathic Board in 1935, by which time he had built up a
large private practice in Morningside, Edinburgh, and the
surrounding southern suburbs of the city. This he carried
on for about 25 years. In 1945, following the death of
Dr Gordon Meikle, he became Chairman of the Company
and found himself inextricably bound up in the fortunes of
the Hydro at a time when great difficulties loomed ahead.
Ultimately he was asked to take over the duties of resident
physician and joint Managing Director with his brother.
This he did in 1949, throwing his whole dynamic energy

into the work, so that, before he died in 1952, he saw the Hydropathic re-established in the public esteem and returning to its erstwhile popularity.

In addition to his duties as resident physician he played the organ for the morning and evening services, and it was he who began the Christmas Eve service of carols, now so popular.

His two recreations were yachting and riding, the former bringing him wide recognition for his seamanship. When living in Edinburgh he rode with the Linlithgow and Stirling and the Lauderdale Hunts, and from Crieff occasionally went out with the Perthshire drag hunt.

Sir James Learmonth, who was then Professor of Clinical Surgery in Edinburgh University, wrote this when Dr Leckie died:

"The sudden and untimely death of Dr Joseph P. Leckie will be sad news for his friends. There is no need to write 'his friends and his old patients', for his patients were one and all his friends. This relationship between patient and family doctor distinguishes the best form of general practice, and that was what Dr Leckie conducted from his house in Cluny Drive—which was also his most hospitable home."

W. Gordon Leckie
O.B.E., B.Sc.

The following extract is from a meeting of the Directors held on 9th March 1948.

Mr W. G. Leckie. The Directors hereby place on record the appointment of Mr Gordon Leckie, O.B.E., B.Sc., as Managing Director of the Company, the appointment to take effect as from 1st June 1948.

Sgd. J. P. Leckie, Chairman. Mary Meikle, Edith P. Meikle, R. J. B. Sellar, A. W. Duncan, Directors.

Mr Gordon Leckie was a typical Leckie—tough, kindly, with unbounded energy and with administrative capabilities trained in the uncompromising conditions of Africa. All those qualities were needed in his position as Managing

Director of the Hydropathic Company at the time of the rehabilitation battle, fought and won in 1948 and 1949.

Educated at George Watson's College, Edinburgh, Gordon Leckie served with the Royal Field Artillery in the First World War, and on being demobilised began to study agriculture at Edinburgh University. After taking his B.Sc. (Agric.) he went off to work in Texas for a year, and on returning joined the Colonial service in Kenya. He served with distinction there for some years, being awarded the M.B.E., and then moved in 1939 to Basutoland as Director of Agriculture. A few years later he received the O.B.E. for his work on soil erosion, and in 1946 was offered the post of Director of Agriculture for Rhodesia but refused and soon after that retired. He came home to Crieff in 1948 to take on another big job.

It was he who suggested to the Board that a resident doctor should be appointed; also someone who could stand in for the Manager, should he be absent. His brother, Dr Joe, fulfilled both these requirements, so the Board teamed them up, how successfully everyone realised within a couple of years.

Mr Leckie too, had inherited the love of sailing and kept a boat on Loch Earn. He was the first Commodore of the Loch Earn Sailing Club. He was also active in the affairs of Crieff Merchants and Hotelkeepers Association, being president for a time.

JOHN LECKIE

When Mr Gordon Leckie took ill at the beginning of June, 1960, his younger son, John, who had been managing the farms on the Hydro estate for a year, was appointed assistant Manager and Secretary. Born in Edinburgh in 1936, he first went to school in Johannesburg, South Africa, and then, after Morrison's Academy and Merchiston Castle School, did his national service in the Navy. Thereafter he proceeded to the East of Scotland College of Agriculture in Edinburgh, where he took his diploma.

With his father's death he found himself very much in the

midst of things, for the Directors, at a meeting just a few weeks later, made him Manager and Secretary.

This was a great responsibility for a young man, but he had the good-will of everyone through their esteem for his father and his family and he has shown that their trust was not misplaced.

If variety is the spice of life then he has it. An ordinary day includes items like the following: Saw Chef. Saw Farm Manager. Phoned re Riding School. Phoned laundry. Saw Joiner. Saw Waitresses. Saw Wages Clerkess. Signed Meikle Trust paper. Visited Bank and Solicitor. Saw Upholsterer. Phoned Dept. of Agriculture. Saw Painter re Ballroom floor. Phoned re Sunday School picnic. Saw Carle.

The entry about the Sunday School picnic indicates one of Mr Leckie's chief outside interests—St. Michael's Church, Crieff, not far from the foot of the Hydro drive—where he is an elder, superintendent of the Sunday School, and a member of the choir. When opportunity offers he is off to Loch Earn with his wife Janet and the children to sail or picnic. A young man whom, on closer acquaintance, one comes greatly to admire.

It has not always been easy to find a suitable assistant to the Manager, but the Board have now had the good fortune to secure the services of just such a person in Mr George Donaldson, a cousin of the Manager and son of the Chairman. A practical farmer, he is able to take a good deal of the weight off the Manager's shoulders in that direction, and is quickly learning the ropes in other ways, too. Mr Donaldson took up duty at the end of 1966. His wife is the Hydro physiotherapist.

OTHER NOTABLES

A remarkably successful group of business men gathered round Dr Thomas Meikle in 1867, among them Mr David Paton, a member of the family who made Paton's "Alloa Yarn" famous before the middle of last century. In 1824, David and his older brother James, hived off from their father and commenced making tweed in the neighbouring town of Tillicoultry, three miles from Alloa. Like their father they, too, were highly successful and at the great Exhibition in London, in 1851, were awarded a gold medal for their exhibits. Both the brothers gave very liberally to the Church for work at home and abroad.

The good work that David began and carried on throughout his lifetime found a most willing successor in his daughter Agnes, the second Mrs Thomas Meikle.

Apart from his fund to give ministers a free holiday, perhaps the most significant gesture by David Paton was his dissent from the appointment of Mr Kennedy, in 1867, as the resident secretary of the Hydropathic Company. Speculation as to what would have happened had he not dissented brings some unhappy ideas. Mr Kennedy, not Dr Meikle, might have held the reins. Even if he had only tried to keep control the position would have been most unfortunate, for Dr Meikle, with all his experience, was not the man to brook interference in his long-laid plans. Had Kennedy been an obstinate man, disaster might easily have overtaken the Company. Paton must have been an extremely shrewd judge of men.

When he died in 1890, the Board minutes stated:

"A Director since the commencement of the Company in 1867, he had materially aided its prosperity in many ways and especially by inviting Ministers and Missionaries to take the benefit of the Estab. for a few weeks every year, in order to improve their health and increase their fitness for work in their various spheres. With singular generosity Mr Paton had done this for 22 years at a cost to himself of upwards of £10,000. The Directors frankly acknowledge their indebtedness to Mr Paton for this service, as well as for his wise counsels at the Board of Management during his lengthened period of service."

Mr George L. Duncan, who married Miss Bessie Meikle, proved an excellent choice as assistant to Dr Gordon Meikle. He had lived and worked overseas, and when he returned home in the summer of 1914 Dr Gordon suggested that he might be made a Director. This was done, and for over 30 years he gave himself unsparingly to the duties of secretary to the Company and assistant to Dr Gordon, whom he survived by just over six months.

Mr Alexander Duncan, his brother, then acted as interim secretary.   Alex. Duncan had been appointed to assist his brother in April 1937, and was made a Director five years later, retiring from the Board in 1949.

Mr John M. Macharg, C.A., served the Company most loyally for 32 years, and his nephew, Mr E. S. Macharg, C.A., carries on the tradition he set.   Although appointed auditor in 1893, John Macharg had been doing the work since October of the previous year, when his predecessor, William McKim, died.   The fee for the work at that time was ten guineas, which included travelling expenses.

Mr A. C. Chalmers, C.A., junior partner to John Macharg, acted as auditor for a period beginning before the Second World War until his death in 1958.   He gave great assistance to the Board throughout the war, when all the problems of troop occupation and then compensation claims arose; also to the Leckie brothers in the crucial years that followed.

The service given to the Hydro by members of this firm seems typical of the attachment which the Establishment draws from so many of its servants.

Appendix II

FACTS AND FIGURES

Any business with interests as varied as this Company's is bound to be full of interrogation marks. How many are there of this? How big is that? And so on, almost to infinity. This appendix answers some of the queries not dealt with in the preceding pages.

How many people stay at the Hydro each year? In the language of the experts, that is, simply, "Arrivals". The answer is around 12,000; but again, the experts do not count that way. The figure they want is—Daily average. This may fluctuate from year to year and indeed, it flows in cycles. Between 1950 and to-day it has gone up enormously —from 139 to the peak year of 1962 when it reached 258·5—very nearly 70 per cent. of the "possible". For the last six or eight years it has been around 250.

For many years after the opening in 1868 the daily average was not regularly calculated and in the minutes of the first 25 years this figure is given only thrice. In 1877 it was 102; in 1885, 80; and in 1886, 77. By 1893 it was 131, and in the two succeeding years 154 and 159, but by the end of the century it steadied at 130 for a few years. In 1910 it was 159 and then began to climb. By 1920 it was up to 227, a figure which was not reached again until 1957. From 1926 the number fell regularly until 1936–37 when, at 141, it touched its lowest since 1908. Within one year of re-opening after the war it was back at that level and then steadily increased.

If you multiply that average of, say, 250 by 365 you get a total of over 90,000. Multiply that again by three and you will have a slight idea of the number of cooked meals served in a year. In fact, including casual visitors and staff it is nearer half a million than 300,000. This involves the washing of about two million pieces of crockery and three and a half million pieces of cutlery.

To provide one course of roast lamb, six carcases are cut up. About two tons of potatoes are used in a week, and for the last 12 years one man has been responsible for removing the "eyes" from somewhere in the region of 16 to 17 million potatoes!

In a year the Establishment goes through six tons of butter, eight tons of sugar, three and a half tons of marmalade 15,000 gallons of milk and 150,000 eggs.

Some 450 morning rolls are made every day, to say nothing of the scones, cakes (700 to 800) and bread baked for afternoon tea and other meals.

The Hydro gardens, as well as being ornamental, provide a good deal of food and many flowers for decoration purposes. There are five acres of vegetable garden, worked in rotation, and giving potatoes, cabbage, cauliflower. Strawberries and raspberries are grown in sufficient quantities to supply the House for a few weeks each year—about 900 lb. and 400 lb. respectively in an average year. Precautions have to be taken to protect these fruit from raiding bands of youngsters. Tomatoes are grown under glass and some 1500 lb. produced in the season.

One of the jobs carried out by Mrs Paterson, House Manageress, is to arrange the flowers displayed in the entrance hall and public rooms. To do this, she visits the gardens and discusses with Mr McInnes the selection of flowers ready for display. One of the greenhouses is given over to forcing some flowers for cutting and also for producing plants which will endure the warm atmosphere inside the Hydro. The six gardeners—there used to be twelve—have also to see to the tidiness of the grounds in general.

The whole Hydropathic estate covers almost 650 acres, and there are three farms with an arable area of almost 350 acres. They are Culcrieff, Dryton (sometimes called Ferntower), and the Colony, and each has its own part to play in the general programme, though the three are run as a unit. At Culcrieff there are some 60 dairy cows, half Ayrshire and half Friesian breeds, giving quality with quantity. In the year they average about 1000 gallons each, at four to five per cent. butter fat.

In July 1965, it was decided to use only pasteurised milk for the Hydro. About the same time the change over to self-feed silage and milking parlour took place. Some 350 to 400 tons of silage are made and 20 tons of hay for the young beasts being fed for beef on the Colony Farm, which is mainly arable. Barley, which is the main feed, is put into a high moisture tower, with glass interior, specially built, and holding 140 tons. "The barley comes out smelling like a distillery," said Mr Archie Osborne, farm manager, "and the cattle love it." About 80 head are fattened at a time.

At Dryton, a new piggery built to replace one flattened by a gale in 1967, houses 50 breeding sows and their progeny of around 400 pigs, which are grown to bacon weight. The Hydro swill is invaluable there.

At Ferntower, the coachhouse and stables are used as a poultry unit, the eggs going to the kitchen and any surplus being sold to the Egg Marketing Board. A few sheep are wintered for a neighbouring farmer.

For a few years broilers were reared in a three-storey building beside Dallerie laundry, but in 1965 fire destroyed the building.

A comparison of the categories of employees, between 1937 and 1967, shows some interesting changes. There is now no resident doctor, but two local doctors attend regularly at the surgery in the Hydro. The office staff, which numbered seven, is now eight. Bathmaids and bathmen have gone, but tablemaids are 16 against 10 in 1937; and six porters and two pages where there used to be five and none. The automatic lift has done away with two liftmen. Housemaids, linenmaids and cleaners are practically the same; 19 housemaids as compared with 20. One man looks after garages and 'bus where there were two garage men and two drivers. There was formerly one billiard marker and one houseman but now there are automatic coinboxes in the billiard room, and there are two housemen.

A big change is seen in the kitchen where three cooks and four apprentices are needed now instead of one cook and no apprentices. But all the ten kitchen maids have vanished along with the two scullery maids. In their place are four kitchen porters; also five pantry maids and four pantry men in place of eleven maids and one man.

There is one electrician and an apprentice compared with three electricians; an upholsterer, with his own workshop, is a new category; plumbers, joiners and painters are the same in number as before—one, three and four. The two masons and three carters have gone, but slater and boilerman remain. By mechanisation the gardening staff has been cut, and there is now no gamekeeper to care for game and other wild life on the Knock.

On the farm six labourers and two ploughmen have given place to a dairyman and three ploughmen-tractormen; two poultrymen have been replaced by one poultryman and a pigman.

At the laundry a manager has taken over from a manageress, and the women operators number 20 against 18 in 1937. No fireman is needed and two vanmen are required as compared with one, and the office and the shop in Crieff each have one employee.

Hydropathic built	1867–68
"New" or West wing built . .	1894
Winter Garden added . . .	1904
Swimming Pool added . . .	1905
dimensions length . . .	53' 0"
breadth . . .	19' 6"
temperature of water .	75 degrees Fahr.
House capacity	about 370 persons
No. of bedrooms	200
No. of employees	150
Laundry—Hydro sends each week in high season	4000 articles
Height of Hydro above sea level . .	440 feet
Height of Indicator on Knock . .	793 feet
Height of Upper Knock . . .	911 feet
Estate extends to	650 acres
No. of private lock-ups for cars . .	58

"TODAY'S HYDRO"

Much has changed in the world since this book was published almost 20 years ago. Changing social standards in the 1960s, the oil crises, inflation and political uncertainty of the 1970s, and the wholesale industrial computerisation and subsequent unemployment of the 1980s have all contributed to a society which has been changing rapidly, and not always for the better.

But through all the changes Crieff Hydro has remained virtually unchanged in character and outward appearance. Twenty years on, many of the same personalities are still there—Paddy the porter still meets arriving guests, and John Leckie still steers at the helm. Many of the regular guests are the same, still making a mental note of their favoured rooms for the same time next year as they pay their bill.

It would be a mistake to think of the Hydro as stagnant during the last two decades, though. Behind the red sandstone walls, and at numerous spots around the grounds, an ambitious series of alterations and additions have been carried out. Perhaps the greatest achievement of the management during these years has been to implement an imaginative policy of change which was vital if the Hydro were to meet the standards expected of a major hotel in the 1980s, while managing to preserve the traditional calmness and character of the place.

There have been casualties in the modernisation. Some of us miss the old brass bedsteads, and the writing must surely be on the wall for the creaking floorboards and gurgling pipes. The daily ritual of afternoon tea, with cake stands loaded with goodies so rich they had to be bad for us has passed, lamented, into history. Despite that, the Hydro is still the same old house upon a hill, as uniquely idiosyncratic as ever, with the same homely atmosphere which has been the cornerstone of its character for 119 years.

When Dr Meikle built the Hydro in 1868, he conceived it as

a resort offering holidays which were, above all, healthy and wholesome. One of the most obvious series of changes has been in the energetic expansion of the sporting facilities. By concentrating on this sector the management have both been true to the founding principles, and economically astute in anticipating the current fitness boom. There are few purpose-built health farms which can boast such an impressive array of health-oriented facilities on offer at nominal charges.

Twenty years on it seems odd to remember a time when squash was a new and rather exotic sport, but that is precisely what it was when the Hydro opened its squash courts in December 1967. The courts were opened by the then Chairman, J. R. Donaldson, and the courts were available not only to guests, but to pupils of Morrison's Academy and the townsfolk of Crieff. The Hydro Squash Club with some hundred members operates out of the courts, which tend to be well used. Numerous tournaments have been played on the courts including, on several occasions, the Scottish Closed Championship.

These courts are now linked to the Sports Hall, probably the most significant investment in the sporting field. Opened in 1980 by Sir Hector Monro, then Minister for Sport, the hall accommodates a vast range of activities, and is a wet-weather facility unique among Scottish hotels.

It can be used as a tennis court, or four badminton courts, thus replacing the old badminton court in the basement, which was popular with families but had become substandard. It is also used for volleyball, basketball, five-a-side football, indoor hockey and yoga. There is a multi-gym downstairs, and a viewing gallery above the main hall.

There are so many sports available at the Hydro now that the management decided to create a family sports club, which would open up the facilities to local citizens. There are now about 300 members in the club, and they ensure that maximum use is made of all the amenities during the quieter periods.

The history of the Hydro is associated with water, of course, but the saga of the "new" swimming pool has not been a happy one. In 1971 the management decided to modernise the old pool down in the basement. Further investigation, however, revealed that it was not going to be significantly more expensive to construct a new one. On the basis that a modern facility is preferable to a patched up old one, it was decided to go ahead with building.

There were problems with the pool almost as soon as it was completed. Basically the architect had designed a pit of concrete blocks encased with a PVC liner. This liner wrinkled, and was replaced. The next one, however, did exactly the same thing before being replaced by a fibre glass liner which also proved unsatisfactory. The pool sprung a leak, and began to lose about 2,000 gallons of water a day, though no-one was ever quite sure what happened to it or where it went.

The pool was scrapped and rebuilt with reinforced concrete, lined with tiles, in the traditional method, and there have been no problems since. The old pool continued to be used by local clubs while all this was going on, but was eventually closed because of costs. It is now used as a store.

And the history of the three all weather tennis courts has been similarly troubled. In the last two decades the courts have had to be resurfaced four times. The most recent application, of a compound called "tennitop", seems to work and it is hoped the old problems of cracked or irregular courts are finished with. There are still two excellent blaes courts.

One of the most recent additions to the sporting line-up is the all weather four-rink bowling green built on the front lawn in 1985. As well as the young and energetic, the Hydro caters for those of mature years who prefer more gentle exercise. The green will allow play all year, and will attract clubs to the Hydro. There are no other hotels in the UK with an all weather surface, and few greens with such a magnificent view. The President of the Scottish Bowling Association, James Allan, opened the green with a rather one-sided match against the Board Chairman, George Donaldson. He later received some expert tuition from Bob Sutherland, former World Bowls Champion.

Slightly further afield is the Culcrieff Golf Course, which closed in 1913 and was resurrected as a "fun" course in 1970. The nine holes are popular particularly with the less expert, and boast some delightfully descriptive names. There is the *Lang Drap*, and the *De'il's Delight*, and the ninth advises the aspiring, but perhaps frustrated, golfer to *Awa' Hame*.

The par-32 course was laid out by John Stark, who for the past 24 years has been the popular and respected professional to the Crieff Golf Club and a good friend to the many Hydro golfers who enjoy the Crieff courses. As it was being laid out an unusual link with the past, in the shape of a "gutty", or old-fashioned leather golf ball was found embedded in a wall. It now crowns a trophy awarded during the annual golf week.

The Hydro course at Culcrieff was opened by one of Scotland's most famous golfers, and former Ryder Cup Captain, Eric Brown, in 1972.

Out at the Loch Earn site, bought in 1957 for £500, there have been developments. Part of the land was sold off as a caravan site, and the rest let out for grazing. The foreshore is popular as a picnic area and a base for water skiing. During the 1960s Lt-Col Archibald Campbell-Crawford of the Seaforth Highlanders leased a section and moved his sailing school over to it from St Fillans. In 1980 the Hydro bought over the school, though the Colonel is still the Sailing Master. It is claimed to be the oldest sailing school in Scotland, and enjoys an excellent reputation.

In the same year the Company bought over six chalets at the other end of the loch at Lochearnhead. These were seasonally popular, but proved to be too small a unit to be run effectively, and so were sold in 1984.

In the grounds of the Hydro there have been many additions, some obvious to the interested guest, others less so. In 1969 John Foster, Director of the Countryside Commission, opened the Nature Trail, based on farm tracks around Culcrieff. The trail was the idea of the Scottish Wildlife Trust, who employed a botanist, a geologist and an ornithologist to lay it out. It is a popular walk with guests, townsfolk and tourists because of the wealth of natural life and remarkable views. The trail extends to 1½ miles and winds its way down from Culcrieff towards the Hosh. It follows "The Lovers' Walk" along the bank of the Turret, striking up through a young plantation to emerge again at the farm steading.

And Culcrieff is also the location of one of the two jogging trails laid out through territory largely owned by the Hydro. There is one two-mile route around the Culcrieff golf course, and another six-miler which follows the south flank of the Knock along behind Ferntower House and down into Gilmerton, and then returns by Monzie.

The Hydro had enjoyed a private supply of milk from its dairy farm at Culcrieff for many years but in 1984 the Directors took the sad decision to close the dairy farm. For some time the Board had been concerned that the farm was not generating profits to match the investment. It was decided to withdraw from farming and ensure a modest return by leasing the farm. The plant and all other mechanical equipment was disposed of, and a fine herd of pedigree Ayrshire cattle was displenished. The grazing rights were let and the Board are still deliberating about the farm's future. It must be appreciated that, whatever the value of the land, the views are priceless, and greatly enjoyed by guests walking down to the Hosh.

Behind the stables is another installation few guests will be aware of, a borehole drilled in 1973. Hotels have their water metered, and it is not simply an item on the rates bill. Given the quantities of water needed in a building the size of the Hydro, it is quite an expensive commodity. It was therefore decided that, as the area was traditionally famed for its water, the possibility of raising some water from within the grounds should be investigated. The source of the original supply tapped by Dr Meikle for Hydropathic purposes, has never been traced, and octogenarian water diviner James Ballantyne from St Andrews was brought in to find a likely source.

Armed with his twigs he confirmed that the entire area was rich in subterranean deposits, and John Leckie recalls the dramatic reaction when Mr Ballantyne wandered behind the stables. So violent was the jerking and twisting that the Manager was quite concerned for the health of his rather elderly consultant! Old James predicted rich deposits of water at 200 ft behind the stables, and his old-fashioned approach was as accurate as a modern geological survey. Water was indeed struck at the predicted depth and place, and it now supplies about one-third of the hotel's water requirements.

Still in the area of the stables, six heated kennels for guests' dogs were built in an outhouse in 1981. The old kennels had been destroyed when part of the stables was burned down in 1968, and during the interim guests who wished to bring their dogs—and there are many—had to leave them in their cars. In the summer the dogs baked, and in the winter they froze. Puppies made a meal of the interior of cars out of boredom, but at no time have dogs been allowed inside the hotel.

But the most obvious change in the grounds is the construction of the chalets in the woods above the tennis courts. In the early 1970s there began a boom in the self-catering sector as cheap package holidays abroad, and rising fuel and labour costs at home, made British hotels a relatively expensive option, particularly for families.

A market for those who wanted to enjoy the facilities of the Hydro without paying for rooms and food clearly existed, and to cater for it the first 11 chalets—the "Bens" and the "Glens" were built. The scheme took off, and the chalets have proved popular, particularly with families. Four "Loch" chalets were later added bringing the total to 15. Another popular venture into the self-catering market has been the letting of Knock Cottage, an old farm cottage beside the first tee of the nine-hole golf course. There used to be a well in the garden, an outside privy and no electricity, but it has been modernised into the Company's most isolated self-catering unit.

In 1968, the Loch Turret Water Board was commissioned to convert Loch Turret into a large dam, the principal purpose being to provide a water supply for Grangemouth. The plan meant that water which had fed the Barvick Dam and powered the Hydro's private hydro-electric supply would now be diverted into Loch Turret. The company was awarded compensation of £11,800 by the Water Board for the loss of this supply.

Up till then the Hydro had operated on a d.c. supply generated at the Barvick. The system depended on a pair of turbines with associated balancers which had to be alternated each day to prevent one set becoming unduly worn. Guests can recall the twice daily ritual of mandatory power-failures lasting a minute or so, while *Old Sandy* the engineer, switched generating sets.

The compensation sum was used to rewire the entire hotel. For a few years previously, the inadequacies of d.c. power had necessitated a partial supply from the national grid to the ground floor and to electric motors. Now the benefits of alternating current—electric shaver points in every bedroom, power points for hoovers and the convenience of unlimited supplies for every conceivable gadget—were freely available throughout the building.

Recently there has been a more vigorous process of upgrading in the bedrooms. Those marvellous brass bed-steads, together with their impossibly saggy mattresses have gone, and most rooms are now centrally heated. Some 75% of the rooms have bathrooms en suite, and soon most of the remainder will be up-graded. The Hydro has 32 "Executive" rooms, which are equipped with a telephone, hairdryer, trouser press and television. Guests are offered complimentary newspapers and bowls of fruit. Despite the conversions, the total number of bedrooms remains at 200. Some of the old rooms have gone to create bathrooms for adjoining rooms, but a skilful manipulation of space has ensured that total accommodation remains constant.

As well as an updating of existing features, improvement within the Hydro has included the addition of new facilities. In 1972 a sauna was built in the basement, conveniently close to the site of the "new" pool. In the same year, and just along the corridor, the cinema was built on the site of the old Turkish baths. It is well-designed with a sloping floor and seats 96. There are no breaks between reels because it has a proper projection room with twin projectors. Feature films are shown twice a week, and provide entertainment on nights when there is no dancing.

The Hydro has always been particularly suitable for the elderly or infirm because all the public rooms are on the ground floor, and most bedrooms are accessible by lift. In 1979 a bathroom for the disabled was installed on the ground floor, featuring fittings designed to help the infirm.

There was a major internal alteration in 1975 with the

opening of the Snack Bar in the Winter Gardens. This has proved a popular amenity with most guests, who find the prospect of three full Hydro meals a day a bit daunting! It brought with it a significant change in tradition, but answered, to an extent, the trend towards fast food and a lighter diet.

Most guests now opt to take lunch at the Snack Bar, although it is always available in the Dining Room. Residents prefer to stick to diningroom lunches, and during conferences and at Christmas and New Year lunches are served in the traditional way.

The Winter Gardens had been refurbished at the same time with modernised heating and pillars lined with tiles and surrounded by pot plants. But the Winter Garden was the scene of further major repairs in 1982 when a storm blew a 30 ft section of the roof off. It ended up on the lawn, and was replaced with a more durable and insulated material.

Just outside, the Loggia, which had previously been open to the elements, was glassed in so that it could be used in all weathers, and the old mosaic floor disposed on in favour of parquet flooring.

A major addition to the facilities of the hotel was the building in 1983 of the Ferntower Suite as a conference centre. Whilst it was recognised that the Company was always dependent to a large extent on family holidays, diversification into other sections of the market was necessary.

For many years the Hydro has been a natural choice for a number of large Christian conferences. The Scottish branch of Gideons International have for nearly 20 years brought their 300 strong conference to the Hydro in November as have the Christian Medical Fellowship. Church of Scotland retreats, groups from Christian Irishman, the Christian Golfers Conference are among many diverse groups to frequent the Hydro. Voluntary organisations like Rotary, Round Table and Soroptimists, Country Dance Societies, Badminton and Squash Clubs are examples of other associations of like-minded people who often choose to spend their annual weekend in the wide open spaces of Crieff Hydro.

Crieff is an ideal place for companies to hold their

conferences, or study groups their seminars, and the restful atmosphere of the town together with the wide choice of recreations available at the Hydro makes attendance at a conference hosted by the Hydro a perk rather than a duty.

The new conference suite features a versatile main hall with stage, bar and toilet block and can accommodate 200 people. It is popular for local functions and wedding receptions as well as business conferences, and has been in steady use since it was built. One advantage is that it attracts people to the Hydro during the low season, thus making sure that the maximum use is made of the hotel at times which might not be most suitable for a family holiday.

The conference suite was opened by Scottish Tourist Board Chairman Mr Alan Devereux who caused great excitement when he arrived on the front lawn by helicopter. In his speech Mr Devereux recognised, and paid tribute to, the philosophy which lies behind the development of the Hydro in the last 20 years. "Much of the success of the Hydro has been a result of its policy of re-investing in the hotel with the result that sports facilities here are widely recognised as among the most comprehensive of any hotel in Britain", he said. "The Hydro has done very well over the years with its value for money policy, and I am sure this will yield good dividends not only in business traffic, but also in the family tourists for which Crieff Hydro is justly famed."

Mr Devereux was spot on in his assessment of the management's philosophy of hotel-keeping, but few people attending the opening ceremony appreciated the other major impact the Ferntower Suite was to have on the life of the Hydro. As well as providing a most up-to-date amenity, it also represented a significant threat to one of the Hydro's most sacred traditions: one of the results of the conference centre was that, for the first time, the consumption of alcohol within the building was formalised.

The lack of a bar for delegates to relax in, tired after a hard day conferring would realistically have been a major draw-back to the success of the suite, and an arrangement was made whereby a bar was imported from the town to cater for conferences and functions. This had a knock-on effect in the

Hydro, and in October that year the management applied for, and were granted, a restricted licence. For the first time ever, a Crieff Hydro wine list was available, and a year later corkage was charged on bottles imported into the diningroom.

The momentous step of introducing the sale of alcohol, even if only in a discreet way in the diningroom, has raised in many minds the question of when or whether an orthodox hotel bar should be installed. Many guests still urge the management to resist what might be seen as a logical progression. Various standpoints are adopted for this plea, but all agree that a full licence would irreparably alter the character of the Hydro. Certainly that atmosphere of homeliness, friendliness and relaxation, of which so many speak and which many more sense, is one which the management wish most jealously to guard.

Whatever happens in the future, one thing is certain; had the Hydro been in other hands since the war, it would by now have had several bars in keeping with any other hotel of comparable size.

Perhaps the reason the Hydro is so good for family holidays is that it is very much a family run establishment. Managing Director John Leckie is descended from Dr Meikle, and related to George R. Donaldson, for many years Joint Managing Director. Both he and George N. Donaldson, the current Chairman are, of course, closely related as son and nephew to Mr Reginald Donaldson, the former Chairman.

George R. Donaldson, cousin of John Leckie, joined the Hydro staff as Assistant Manager in 1966 when Mrs Barbara Leckie retired. As a farmer it was natural that he should assume responsibility for the farms and the Estate in general but his warm personality endeared him to many visitors to the Hydro, especially if they played golf. George is a low handicap golfer and he introduced the June and August Golf Weeks, the latter the high-point of the summer season when *regulars* make their annual pilgrimage from all over Britain to compete for numerous trophies, including the Culcrieff Gutty. George was the inspiration for the Hydro's 9-hole course and for the extension of the Crieff Course to provide 27 holes. His wife Elizabeth became the Hydro Physiotherapist, a department she ran for 22 years, and her artistic talents found expression in the floral decorations which have been such a feature of the Hydro foyer. In the foyer too, she established the Hydro Gift Shop, now a permanent ingredient of the services provided for guests and an opportunity for contact with guests—so vital in as large a place as the Hydro.

The *family* tradition was fostered too by Mr and Mrs Everett who came from semi-retirement in England to serve the ethos of this Scottish hotel they had visited so often. Mr Everett, an Accountant, overhauled the somewhat out-dated office procedure, played the organ for Sunday evening services and generously gifted 100 hymn books for use in the Drawing Room. He and his wife played bridge, ran outings in their car and in many other ways befriended residents during their stay.

George Donaldson's withdrawal from day-to-day involvement with the Hydro in favour of farming coincided with a serious slump in the traditional holiday trade in the early 80s. Norman Murray, who had run the Bruntsfield Hotel in Edinburgh for many years, was recruited as Hotel Manager. His nose for the commercial market and flair for functions of every sort found expression in Crieff. These valuable ingredients coincided with the newly built conference facilities and a conscious marketing effort to fill the empty beds during the quieter periods.

But the marketing professions, so much in vogue in the challenging climate of the Eighties, recognise the need for individualism and unusualness in a business image. All the amiable eccentricities, all the abiding but unprofitable traditions (such as the Sunday evening service or the absence of a bar) should by the standards of a normal hotel have been regularised. And with the traditions would have gone much of the charm. And when the charm went, so too would many of the loyal families, couples and individuals who generation by generation have enjoyed it just the way it is for more than a century.

The Hydro is about service, tradition, and friendship as much as profit, and it is precisely these features which make the Hydro unique. There are many large, luxurious, country-house type hotels in Britain, but there is only one Hydro. No one would wish to see it turned into just another *resort hotel*.

Another characteristic of the management is the length of time most have been associated with the Hydro. John Leckie has been there since 1960 and his dedication and imagination over these years has engendered the growth of unrivalled sporting facilities and major refurbishment. He, like both George Donaldsons, has been brought up in the spirit of the place. This tradition of long service, and even longer association with the Hydro, has ensured unusually close association with the staff, many of whom have been there just as long. There have, for instance, only been four Chefs since 1907.

A system of long service awards was established in 1967, which provides for a special payment to staff who have been there for 10 years, and another payment for every five subsequent years. Many of the staff are well-known to the regulars, and are regarded more as friends than servants.

The best known of these must be Charlie Wilson, who has been leading his Blue Ribbon Dance Band in the ballroom for the last 30 years. Although not actually an employee of the Hydro, Charlie has been the common factor in the local ensemble, as singer, accordionist, organist and saxophone player. He has done much to popularise country dancing among the younger generations, who always seem happy to re-peat the "Duke of Perth" endlessly until the exhausted Charlie waves them away and insists they "Go awa an sit doon".

Charlie's wife Edith was until recently a waitress in the Dining Room, much sought after by guests who came to know her over the years, and enjoy her cheery banter and crisp efficiency.

Nursery Supervisor Marie Pryde can trace her family history back through the Hydro's staff books. She is the third generation to work there: her great-uncle, Willie Duff, was the first baker and her grandmother, Anne Duff, a house-table maid. Marie has a remarkable memory for names, and frequently astounds guests by remembering them, and their grown-up children, years later.

Another pair noted for their facility with names are

long-serving porters Frank Dunbar, recently retired after 40 years service, and Paddy Hallissy. Paddy has been a porter since 1952, and was for many years the resident piper, playing around the dining room and corridors at New Year and not infrequently being waylaid with a hearty dram.

Paddy used to be accompanied on the Hogmanay march around the dining room by another Crieff legend, Chef Sandy MacGregor, who died in 1978. He came to the Hydro after the war and became one of the cornerstones in shaping its resuscitation. He loved to leave the hot plate and move around the dining room chatting to guests who always enjoyed his amusing repartee. He introduced the annual procession round the dining room on Hogmanay, culminating in the tossing of the turkey—a ritual which was eagerly awaited and not always entirely successful! He was a noted golfer and was captain of Crieff Golf Club for three years.

Sandy MacGregor gathered round him a loyal staff, some of whom are still there.

Hans Protze, originally from East Germany, is the baker behind the breakfast rolls which have been firm favourites with guests since 1952. Regular guests may have noticed he is now catering for the trend towards brown flour, and the increasing emphasis on fibre in the diet.

Boilerman Joe Burke started out as an assistant baker before moving to his present post. He witnessed the demise of coal-fired boilers and their replacement with oil-fired *package* boilers which have worked steadily for 20 years. Current Sous Chef Eddie Stewart started as a dishwasher in 1953 before graduating to the kitchen, rising to be third chef under Sandy MacGregor.

Bennie McLaughlan, who came in 1953 is, like Eddie, a Glaswegian. He is now in charge of cleaning the silver. In his spare time he acts a chief projectionist, screening films twice weekly in the cinema.

The Hydro's plumber rejoices in the singularly apt name of Bert Watters, and has been a stalwart since 1961, never flinching from the most unattractive blockage or underground enigma. In his time private bathrooms have increased from 2 to 150 and gas fires have almost entirely given way to central heating.

Margaret Mackintosh came from Nairn in 1950 and married Bill Barron, the original silverman. After his untimely death, she remarried and since then has serviced rooms on the ground floor west wing. Agnes Howell, Cathy Moran and Bunty Black are three of the longest serving housemaids, having been at the Hydro since 1949, 1955 and 1959 respectively, and have served under Head Housekeepers, Mrs McCartney, Mrs McKinlay, Miss Robb and Miss Campbell.

Isobel McCabe came from Lanarkshire in 1965 and later married a Crieff painter. She has always worked in the Linen Room and as an expert seamstress spends much of her time repairing sheets, tablecloths and linen. One of the Hydro's four painters is Robert Kehoe who has painted virtually every corner of the building since 1963. His daughter Christine was a receptionist before her marriage.

Out in the grounds Head Gardener George McInnes retired in 1986 after an amazing 50 years. For 35 years he recorded the rainfall at the Hydro for the Meteorology Office, and was awarded the Long Service Medal with Bar by the Royal Horticultural Society before retiring.

It is unlikely that many of them will still be serving when this book is next updated, but by then some of the younger members of staff will be elevated by length of service into the respected positions they now hold.

But if the Hydro has prospered during the last 20 years, the credit must ultimately go to those who have directed its affairs from the top. A round up of these years would not be complete without mentioning some at least of those who have steered the Company on a course of success.

Mr J. R. Donaldson, while still Chairman of the Company, died in September 1974. His successor, Sir Malcolm Knox, paid this tribute: "Mr J. Reginald Donaldson has been a Director of this Company since 1949 and its Chairman since 1952, died on 24 September. During all that time he missed a Board Meeting only twice and then he was in hospital suffering from the onset of the illness against which he made a gallant struggle for two years. His fellow Directors hereby place on record their profound gratitude to him for all he did for the Company, for his wise and constant guidance and for his massive contribution to the Company's prosperity. At the same time, conscious of a severe loss which is personal and not merely official, they record their admiration and affection for their leader and friend, and their deep sympathy with his widow and all members of his family".

After Mr Donaldson's death, Sir Malcolm Knox, by then retired as Principal of St Andrews University, assumed the Chair. He had been a Director since 1960 and had given a great deal of his time and business skill to the affairs of the Hydro. His penetrating intellect and administrative experience were invaluable assets in coping with the many difficult decisions which the Board had to face.

Sir Malcolm retired as Chairman in 1976, and from the Board in June 1979, and he was succeeded by Mr Robert Mickel, a local solicitor, whose father had also been a Director of the Crieff Hydro. Mr Mickel was to be Chairman of the Company for eight eventful years. When he stood down in 1984, shareholders were told "His sound judgement has led the Board to make wise decisions resulting in profitable trading, rising dividends and a strong balance sheet—and an increase in the book value of the Company from £375,000 to £875,000—during his term of stewardship".

Mr George N. Donaldson was appointed Chairman to succeed Mr Mickel—who remains a Director—and they, along with John Leckie as Managing Director, George R. Donaldson and Robert Simpson—a well respected and successful farmer at Duchlage in Crieff, constitute the present Board of Directors.

Mr Edgar Macharg, nephew of the Company's original Auditor, served the Company for 30 years. His indefatigable energy resulted in long night hours during the twice yearly audit of the Company's books, lasting a week at a time. Time was always found, however, for an afternoon's golf with Chef MacGregor or George Donaldson. His retirement was marked in 1982 by a dinner in his honour and by warm tribute to his diligence and great personal involvement in the affairs of the Company.

If these and others were on the bridge piloting the Company to prosperity, then at the helm since 1960, when he took over the management on the death of his father, is John Leckie. The dedication, skill and sheer hard work he has put into the running of the Hydro have been in very large measure responsible for its success during these 26 years. He has presided over the remarkable growth in the Hydro amenities and sporting facilities and has masterminded the development of the chalets and the major refurbishment and alterations in the Hydro itself. Now that their family has grown up John's wife, Janet, is playing an increasing and valuable part in the Hydro's affairs and in particular she looks after the chalets and is responsible for the redecoration of the rooms. In addition it is she who arranges the flowers in the Hydro. Even leisure time has been put to good use and countless guests have good reason to be grateful to the Leckies for the opportunity to first sample the pleasures of water-sport of one sort or another on Loch Earn.

The last 20 years have been a period of unprecedented growth. But there can be no doubt that there will be further additions, improvements and refinements in the next 20 years, and the next chronicler of the Hydro will have a busy time of it keeping track of all the doings at the place.

But change and refinement are a process the staff are accustomed to at the Hydro. As one faithful retainer put it as he was sent off to do another job—"Ye'll ne'er get rust on your tackety boots working at this place!"

Long may it continue.

INDEX

N.B. The Index does not make reference to the updated Foreword or the new chapter "Today's Hydro". . .